LOVE AND INDUSTRY

A MIDWESTERN WORKBOOK

LOVE AND INDUSTRY

A MIDWESTERN WORKBOOK

Belt Publishing

Printed in the United States of America
First edition 2023
1 2 3 4 5 6 7 8 9

ISBN: 978-1-953368-58-4

Belt Publishing
13443 Detroit Avenue, Lakewood, OH 44107
www.beltpublishing.com

Cover art by David Wilson
Book design by Meredith Pangrace

TABLE OF CONTENTS

FLYING THE FLANNEL

I bought my first blue plaid flannel at Kmart—so it must have been 1987 or '88, when I was a junior in high school in small-town Illinois. Flannel is any fabric softened by brushing its fibers out into a fuzz called a "nap," and the first plaid flannel patterns were woven in sixteenth-century Wales from the bluish, white, brown, and black wool of a muted rainbow of sheep. My cheap flannel was cotton with the plaid pattern printed on, and, therefore, it was a copy of a copy of a copy, as removed from the original as a Xeroxed image of a photograph.

I sort of knew my high school flannel was fake because I'd seen other plaid shirts—sold in upscale outdoorsy stores—that were made from real thread in different colors woven together. I liked the thinness of mine, like I like other fake things I was born into, things I shouldn't like but do, things that remind me of the Midwest: Hamburger Helper, mac and cheese from a box, fries from the freezer—food extruded, mass-produced, and wrapped in plastic.

I don't think flannel would mind that its essence has been copied. Flannel forgives.

In the 1980s Midwest, flannel typically meant metal dudes, but the metal dudes had earned their flannel from their blue-collar fathers. A flannel at school instead of a button-down meant, *I want to be comfortable, and this is my dad's,* and, *Yes, it's worn and dirty, and that's me, so fuck you.* We all stole clothes from our dads and brothers. That was just how we dressed. Or, more precisely, it was how *they*—our fathers and brothers— dressed because it made sense for work. And then we copied them. I was using this fabric that was so soft to cross over into something, either into boy-land or into a land that was rough: the land of working with one's hands, the land that was invisible and fading as the Rust Belt withering around us.

The first time I wore my flannel to school, I was hiding the tiniest of rebellions. It covered a T-shirt upon which I'd hand-lettered, with fabric paint and a toothpick, a message about the perils of nuclear war. I'd copied the quote from a library book, Jonathan Schell's *The Fate of the Earth*: "We look away. We remain calm. We are silent. We hope that the holocaust won't happen." Kids in my high school did not wear T-shirts with slogans meant to save the world. My farm-town high school of 2,800 students was known primarily for its football team and its strict discipline, which might have made it the perfect *Red Dawn* epitome of the Reagan years. A Che Guevara shirt, if anyone had known the image or what it meant, would have earned a suspension or a busted lip. So I covered my DIY Schell quote with a flannel for extra safety. Flannel was an envelope, and my sternum was a shy billboard I could flash and hide. Flannel bulked me up, hid my body, yet let me choose when and what to reveal.

I remember hunching my shoulders as I walked near the school office, pulling the flannel around me. I got into trouble in those days, like everyone did. I was once threatened with suspension for asking why we didn't have a school newspaper, but I was also an anxious honors student, a good girl. I walked toward the science hall and the auto shop, where the stoners and shop guys hung out—also decked in flannel. We were deep in the corn grid of the Midwest, where it ran up against the grid of south Chicagoland. If there was a map to our future options, it might well have been as squared and segmented as the intersecting lines across our backs: we were to head straight, turn only at right angles, and not expect too much in the way of variation.

Years later, a boyfriend would tell me I should show my body more, that I hid in baggy jeans and big shirts. But that boxiness was freedom. My flannel came from the men's section of Kmart, helping me return to my tomboy roots after a few years of spending my money on bizarre 1980s Coca-Cola logo apparel, Ocean Pacific T-shirts, and over-zippered jackets and shirts. Flannel appeared as a passageway out.

A few boys and girls had started wearing the neat new-wave fashion of pressed shirts with the top button closed at the throat. With this style, boys and girls looked the same, with blotches of lipstick and eyeliner on whitened faces. I loved the Cure, but my body wanted more of a mess. The electronica of Erasure and the Pet Shop Boys and their neatly composed outfits lived in a clean space, and next door was where we flannel-clad kids lived, inside a punk roar that arrived to collide with the ocean of blues-to-rock-to-metal riffs we'd been raised in. And the tent that sheltered this area where the two waves met, at least in my tiny corner of the Midwest, was flannel. In the music, we saw ourselves as something, and flannel came to stand for whatever that something was. It let us see ourselves.

I must have seen flannel stretched across the shoulders of rock stars whose cassettes I bought—Yo La Tengo and the Pixies and the Replacements. I leaned in to listen and watch their images on television, hoping to decode in the videos of MTV's

120 Minutes any signal that might lead me to a future beyond the girl writhing on the hood of a car to a Whitesnake song.

Flannel hid a woman's shape, yet it also revealed as we pushed our breasts against its grid. Inside flannel's tent, I could pause. I became a cipher, a vertical invocation of not dressing to please those around me. I had safety because I was one of a herd, and yet I was opting out. Days in flannel were the days in which my body would not be sized up nor my energy drained by inventing appeasing responses to flirting and banter. I was dressing for my own comfort, and in a roomy flannel, I could actually breathe. My chest could expand, I could slouch, and my body itself could enjoy the feeling of being alive without having each breath be a performance for others. These breaths in flannel did not save me, but they accompanied me into adulthood with the whisper that such a space was possible—a space where I could be only for myself.

———————

Flannel entwines with another vanished smell: the particular intense plastic odor of unwrapping the shrink-wrap from a new cassette, the slight give as you fold open the case, the cassette itself so new it almost seems moist, just born. You pop it into the cassette player on the dashboard and it speaks, it sings, while you slip out the liner notes, folded over and over like a note passed in school, to read the lyrics, the acknowledgments, the secret messages meant only for you in the shelter of your dirty car. I purchased my first Sex Pistols cassette at a Sam Goody's in a Joliet mall when I was in eighth grade. A few weeks earlier, a semi-scary boy in my class held his headphones up to my ears and let me hear the melodic screaming. I listened to it and immediately loved it, which made no sense, because I had also been a devoted fan of Huey Lewis and the News. But the screaming and tonal almost-chanting about anarchy opened a flower in my chest I had not known was closed. It wasn't that I wanted to be the boy who played me the tape. I wanted to be fierce; I wanted the map for that. I loved that angry sound, which cut through the sleepiness of Precious Moments figurines and cheerleader tryouts and student council and eyeshadow and Love's Baby-Soft. So I became a mathlete who loved the Dead Kennedys.

A few years ago while in the car running errands, my husband, Cliff, flipped through the dial and landed on a right-wing, hate-spew radio station. He listened to them to hear their arguments and obsessions, to keep tabs, but I often found myself yelling at them as if they could hear me, like a dog barking at a UPS truck. On that day, the host, Andrew Wilkow, made a comment that he was fond of punk music.

I sat up straight and pounded the dashboard with my fist and yelled at the radio, "You can't talk about punk rock!"

My head flamed with rage as if my nation had been invaded. I could almost feel the tiny particles of spit winging their way toward the radio and the windshield as I shook my head like a dog flapping its jowls. My husband looked over with his eyebrows up. I sat back, wide-eyed. We both laughed nervously, regarding me as if I had grown another head out of my forehead: the punk rock nationalist.

Who *can* talk about punk rock? I explained to my husband that punk has never been right-wing, but of course I am wrong. I only have to remember scowling at the skinheads with the red shoelaces, pogoing at shows in Minneapolis. Yet I know I am also right.

I myself have sneered at the grid encasing punk culture, if it even exists anymore—the conformity in nonconformity. Whatever. Screw punk if it would ever tell me I wasn't punk rock. I will fight anyone for the right to be part of a nation that never wanted to be a nation.

———————

Flannel is now written into music history wrong; it waves as a sort of flag for the broad swath of music known as "grunge." Grunge was not a name we chose, though. There was "punk," and there was "alternative," and there was "metal." Bands like Soundgarden and Pearl Jam and Nirvana were "Seattle" but also kind of "metal" (Soundgarden) or "punk" (Nirvana). They all fit loosely under the term "alternative," which I would argue encompassed any band that appeared late at night on MTV's *120 Minutes*. I could be wrong about the boundaries of punk and grunge, but I know the timeline: I started wearing the flannel I bought from Kmart around 1987. The music that would later be identified as "grunge" ruled from 1983 to 1993, according to Michael Lavine, who cowrote the 2009 book *Grunge* with Thurston Moore.

Wikipedia says of flannel shirts: "Popular grunge bands like Nirvana and Pearl Jam us[ed] them as one of their trademarks of their shaggy look." If I weren't such a slacker, I might sign in as an editor to correct three errors in that sentence. Those bands didn't think of themselves as grunge, and they didn't *use* shirts in any way. Lavine writes that flannel wasn't packaging: "that was just how they dressed." The shirts were not trademarks, which would indicate the desire to develop a brand and sell a product with an image. As Kyle Anderson writes in *Accidental*

Revolution: The Story of Grunge about Nirvana's video for "Smells Like Teen Spirit," "One of the things that stands out is the fact that Kurt is wearing a flannel shirt. Soon flannel would become a generic identifier for all the kids who were embracing 'slacker' culture, but that wasn't true when 'Smells Like Teen Spirit' was made."

The math is backward, at least for that girl standing in the front entryway of a high school in New Lenox, Illinois. Nirvana's video came out in 1991. At the time, I'd been wearing flannel studiously for four years, as had many kids around me. The wrongness of the timeline undermines that tender time in my life when I was trying to map out where I fit, in a place that is often invisible and among a group of people who are often thought to mean not much at all.

In *Grunge*, Lavine and Moore write that the era embraced slacker culture, but few cultural retrospectives mention the backdrop of the bombs raining on Iraq during Operation Desert Shield, which lasted from August 2, 1990, to January 17, 1991. Analysis of "slacker" or Generation X culture rarely captures the protests against the Gulf War or raises the question of whether young people felt hopeless after the Reagan years, in the face of a shock-and-awe war as televised spectacle—in other words, what slackers wanted to drop out of.

The United States continued its legacy of geographic protectorates in order to ensure its supply of oil from the Middle East. In the early 1990s, we shipped our young people to Iraq with their Pearl Jam and Nirvana cassettes—who knows if any of them brought flannels with them? Those of us back home who weren't fighting watched from our living rooms as Dan Rather broadcast with a backdrop of stunning traces of light from the dropping bombs. We pulled our flannels tight around our shoulders that winter, not knowing that the word "flannel" could also be a verb, meaning "to talk evasively to; flatter in order to mislead." We came into flannel in a time of war, as the Cold War bled seamlessly into endless intrusions in the Middle East. We stood on street corners with our wilting signs for peace in the driving snow. Before the internet, we watched the evening news for coverage of our carefully planned demonstrations and huge marches, and we saw nothing. We learned how to write press releases that we faxed off into the void. We were called slackers because we dressed down and wanted to opt out, but we only slacked in depression and exhaustion after screaming to be heard. My generation cried into our flannel shirts, understanding that childhood had been over for a long while.

The nice thing about a cheap flannel shirt was that, for a time, it was all you needed: nightgown, shirt, jacket, handkerchief, napkin, robe, sweater. Flannel was my animal skin.

When I left home for college, flannel's muted colors allowed me to blend into various new flocks. First, I joined the neo-hippie geology majors and environmental activists whose flannels were often of the thicker woven kind, meaning a person came from a different home, a different place, a different bank account, and a different view of the world.

Then I used the same flannel to pass into the punk rock and alternative crowds at music shows in Minneapolis, whose members wore authentically cheap copies and would never have been caught dead in a woven flannel. Finally came the anarchists, whose women wore tank tops with no bras and, of course, a flannel over the top.

The second and third groups did something audacious: they used their sleeves as the ends of a knot, securing the flannel around their middles. The blue jeans of my twenties were practically falling off my ass, more holes than denim fabric, but my superpowers—what little I had—were contained in the girdle of a flannel, its sleeves knotted around my waist, its bulk hanging behind me like a cape. Knotting the sleeves in front of my pelvis felt as natural as tying my shoes. The extra layer of fabric around my hips felt like protection, and the girl I was at twenty could tie a flannel around her waist and rock. E. T. Renbourn writes in "The History of the Flannel Binder and the Cholera Belt" that "girding the loins was also preparation for activity and for war." Warriors would wrap themselves in waist sashes that exist today in the form of the cummerbund, that strange tuxedo accessory that comes from the Persian "*Kamberband*," which means "loincloth."

The girdle or belt divided "the pure upper half from the impure lower half of the body," according to Renbourn. I don't think I felt my nether regions to be impure, but accentuating the hips draws attention to curves and, thus, to sex. A flannel tied at hip level served to inadvertently maximize curves, accentuating one's hips in contrast to the waist, like a low-budget bustle.

Renbourn describes the sacredness of belts and binders in protecting the body's vulnerable middle: "It may be that, in the subconscious mind, the flannel belt has become symbolic of duty, of a tight rein over the basic instincts, and of protection from a hostile environment."

"Flyin' the Flannel" is a song and an album by the band fIREHOSE. I flailed and headbanged to it and other songs at their show in Minneapolis, maybe in 1992, and as soon as the club got steamy with sweat, I took my flannel sleeves and over-undered them into a knot at my pelvis. Maybe Dinosaur Jr. was headlining, and maybe I pulled a muscle in my neck from headbanging and pogoing. Afterward, we stepped into the cold, frozen and heated and steaming and laughing, shining under the streetlamps.

Sweating and headbanging at First Avenue in Minneapolis, you could soak through a tank top or T-shirt, and the flannel around your waist would even get soaked with the sweat that poured from your body in a whirling mosh pit flung with glistening limbs. There was the joy of collision with no obligation. You could be physical, ecstatic, and it wouldn't matter for a second that you were a girl. We danced with our elbows out to jab muscled assholes who got too violent. We laughed admiringly at stories about girls who brought hatpins to the pit to poke at jerks who thought dancing was Fight Club.

Now flannel is quaint, old enough to be a set piece, like wearing a monocle. A piece on *McSweeney's Internet Tendency* entitled "List: Positions of the Kama Sutra for Midwesterners" makes fun of people from the region for wearing flannel "unironically."

After I read that, I took a good five minutes to flip through all of my days in flannel, to try to imagine them as an ironic performance. I became convinced, first, that the writer of the piece didn't understand what irony actually means. I wrote a long screed about irony and then erased it.

That bit of *McSweeney's* satire assumes we can choose either ignorance and "natural" behavior or conscious irony. I read in it the idea that a certain segment of the country shoulders a garment without knowing that the garment speaks, that the garment is a sign. I believe, instead, that in my high school days, even those who wore it for warmth and functionality knew it was a kind of flag. We chose it as a secondary nation—but not for the sake of irony. We chose it out of love. Copying is not always irony. Copying can be tribute. Copying is pastiche, making something new from what you have. Copying is reaching and creation.

If my flannel shirt could have sung a song, that song would have been gridded like the fretboard of a guitar, a song crisscrossed with strains of social class and region and the grit of country or city mixed with its opposite—kids trying to create art and doing things that maybe their working- and lower-middle-class parents would freak out about. Yet those kids, if I am right, might have said that flannel did not mean making fun of where they came from. Instead, flannel was used to make something new without jettisoning the markers of class and work.

If there was irony at all in a flannel as it was worn by these bands, by my friends, and by me, I believe the shirt and its lumberjack reputation turned into a question when it was worn by Fugazi, who sang songs urging people to wake up and to also stop treating girls like shit, or by the Dead Milkmen, with their plaintive mayhem, or even by Kurt Cobain, with his dresses. The question was whether there could ever be a different kind of man than the men our boys were being raised to become.

These days, my flannels rest like old dogs in a bin in my closet. I don't wear them much. Sliding my arm through a flannel sleeve is tiring, like riding time backward. The shirts have become exhausting friends who show up from the past and demand we raise hell, live on the edge.

I shake out my favorite one on an overcast day when I have forgotten who I am. It comforts but also urges me to be the woman I dreamed I would become. The flannel wants me to live the collective, to be punk rock. It wants me to reveal and to hide, to choose when to be seen. It holds up a cutout of the shape of a girl: all I dreamed I would be and all I was at twenty.

When I slip it on, I feel the cape too, and the loins girded for battle, a reminder of fully inflated lungs, elation, and anarchistic joy. I am that girl then, the one who might not have imagined how the grid and the shape of the future would adhere to her body.

MY MEN

There is a gruffness in their voices and an impulsive frustration at the core of them, the men who made my sense of the word "man." They fed me crackling fried pork rinds and hunks of summer sausage in the back of a gray-blue van as we rolled from Illinois down some two-lane highway in West Virginia or northern Arkansas, with Mom drinking a Tab, talking on the CB, and singing her heart out to ABBA or to the Eagles' "Desperado." These men were weathered to a red-brown, with tattoos or missing fingers, missing teeth, and some of them got rowdy and regrettable when they drank. They nursed lit cigarettes or sucked plugs of tobacco. They butchered cows, and I ate the sweet, earthy, smoked blood sausage they made with their hands. I marveled at the cars they painted, the fence posts they sunk, the sheds they built. When they were mad, you ran or prayed, though there were ways they could be tricked. Feminism was funny to those men, but a broad who was tough enough to tell them to go straight to hell earned herself some respect. Their smell was tobacco on skin, Jim Beam rising from a sunburn, pine and clay dirt, the warm vinyl of an old car, and a spray of WD-40.

I kept looking for a man who smelled like that.

———————

Frank was a tall, sweet, foul-mouthed rebel with bleached-blonde hair from a poor coal town in northern England, and I almost married him so he could get his green card. Then I met Ian, a socialist organizer with an eight-year-old son. Ian had been a carpenter for years, and he borrowed gas money from me on our first date. Later, I bought groceries with food stamps he had traded for beer. I paid his overdue $250 gas bill and the rent. He asked me to marry him before he'd gotten divorced from the mother of his child. He never did take care of that divorce, but I was roped into a romance of chaos, of being the island of calm in some man's wild life.

In between, before and after, there have been the others: men with more money, with calmer and more composed stories, women with well-stocked bookshelves and questions, an array of dates without children, homemade tattoos, and nightmarish scars. Frank and Ian, though, are among the ones who would rivet me to the sidewalk if I happened to run into them, the ones who have left the deepest marks. It's probably because they remind me of other men, of the first men I knew.

———

My men sit with their forearms on the bar or kitchen counter, twist their mouths and glare, talk about this or that bastard at work, the specific problem at hand, how we have gotten ourselves into this pickle that was obviously some ee-jit's fault. I thought an ee-jit was a specific beast, a demonic abbreviation—E. Jit—until I realized it's ableist Arkansas for "idiot," not a hill-dwelling hunchback with silver eyes.

It is 8:14 p.m., and everything will be all right just because they are so angry right now. We wait on their every word, silently chewing the insides of our cheeks. They have the answer. Because they don't say much, every word has more weight to bear and rings true, even when it lies.

My men do not talk about their scars. You can be flesh and blood or wife-to-be to these men and not know about their stories, the major events that formed them as they are. The past is a train of mistakes barreling into the day. Even admitting that last week existed is treason. You try to piece together their stories with second- and third-hand information. A memory repeated once round the block is a treasure, a clue.

When, at five, I showed my grandfather the sky-blue shell of a robin's egg I'd found on his Arkansas farm, he smashed it in my palm. "Dreck," he said—"dirty" in German—and I ran back to the house, terrified at this tiny shock. He had piercing, light blue eyes and a waxed handlebar mustache. He was a butcher who was missing the top third of two fingers on his right hand, from when he'd caught them in a meat grinder. At the wake after his funeral, I sat under an end table in that flagstone house on the hill and dared not breathe so no one would notice me, so I could soak up the stories as people got drunk and laughed and went around the room late into the night, talking about what a son of a bitch he had been, about the way he kicked his children, and about other dark stories that would have to wait for other wakes.

Dad came from a family where all four of his sisters went into the convent. They were married to Christ, so at least they had somebody who didn't bother them too much and was never late with the rent.

My dad is one of my grandfather's sons. My Uncle Herb, who has passed away, was the other. Uncle Herb was a career Air Force mechanic who looked like a human stick of tattooed beef jerky because of all the time he'd spent outside and because of all his partying. He was both an utter asshole and a sweetheart. His wife left him and melted down all the jewelry he'd given her into a "divorce ring." She moved across the ocean to get away from him before moving back into his house.

Dad is Dad. I wonder what it felt like for him to sell pie tins door to door when he knew he belonged in medical school. I don't know the answers to any of his questions. These are my men. They have often been more like storms than actual people you can have relationships with.

———————

My men clean up real good. Unused to suits, bashful of themselves in tailored lines, their shoulders support a suit coat, and you realize how tall, how strong they are. Their freshly shaved necks and cheeks look anxious and raw; their rough wrists grazed with white cuffs look grateful for a rest in that shiny fabric. You know the downside to a suit. It means a celebration, which means a few drinks too many, which means a scene later you might like to forget but of course you won't because you are the elephant girl. So you remember those suit moments almost as if the suit created the evil comment, the slurred speech, and then you distrust anything tailored. You look forward to dressing up and to special occasions for weeks, but no one ever seems to notice your new earrings or shoes—then again, how could they? They are just trying to navigate all the pieces of their own outfits, to steer around the tables and chairs and do what they are supposed to. And at the end, your nylons are ripped and you want to ball up that dress in the trash, and so for the next special occasion, you buy a new one, like a Kleenex, to start fresh and not wear something cursed with last time.

I was in college and home on break. My Uncle Herb was living with my parents. One night, he sat at the kitchen counter, solidly and amiably drunk and smoking Pall Malls. A squat, round glass sat in front of him on the counter, with melting ice cubes and a layer of Jim Beam coating the bottom. He was wearing a short-sleeved T-shirt, and he floated a gravelly proposal that he and I go have a beer at the White Horse Tavern down next to the grocery store. Mom was standing near the sink, putting dinner leftovers into Tupperware, and she nixed the scandalous proposition immediately.

"It's late. Why don't you guys just stay in instead?"

So we sat there and talked about tattoos because I had just gotten one, a mild-mannered lizard on my shoulder. I had a little Jim Beam in a glass with lots of water. I asked him about the eagle tattoo on his forearm. He told me stories about four or five of them all over his torso and arms, each one connected to a base in his Air Force career.

I poked at a wedge of inked skin, the blue lines blurry with age, showing under the seam of his T-shirt. He pulled up the sleeve. I saw the four splayed arms of a squared-off cross, inked in dark blue and then outlined.

"That's a fucking Iron Cross," I said, my heart sinking into the soles of my feet.

He smiled at me, slowly revealing his teeth.

"We're German," he said. My grandparents had emigrated from Germany to Arkansas between the wars, when Uncle Herb was a baby and before my dad was born. "That's where I was born. German pride." He stretched out the word "pride" to "praaahd," the same way my dad did when he drank and sounded more Arkansas.

"That's fucked up," I said. Without Jim Beam's help, I never would have opened my mouth to swear at him.

We looked at each other, and he raised his eyebrows just a touch, opened his eyes, as if to say, "Not bad." He smiled at me, giving me a look like, *ooh, you wacky college girl, what are they putting in your head up in that private school in Minnesota?*

"That's where your family is from, girl."

"But that's an Iron Cross. Like the Nazis," I said.

"I ain't no Nazi," he said, shaking his head at me.

The art of my men is not collected. They can throw together a new shed out of whatever plywood and shingles happen to be lying around. They can sand and prime a beater car, spray on coat after coat of candy-red paint until the metal looks good enough to bite. They can stand on a soapbox and organize a union, make a flyer. They have burned beautiful, broad, black skid marks in perfect arcs and lines on fresh patches of pavement.

In the eyes of my men lives a wild-eyed child, and I would like nothing more than to please him. I see a little boy's confusion when things go wrong, an innocence that makes me unpack another of my red glass hearts and slide it skittering down the bar toward him. My men close their brown fingers carefully around it, look at it the way they study a lock that won't unstick, confused and studious. And then they smile, show a bit of their teeth, and crinkle their eyes, and I know that it will be OK if a face like that can change.

I want to see the whole story unfold, wild to sane. I want the impossible drama from beginning to end, want to see a movie where a man in a Bruce Springsteen song ends up understanding the song and singing it, becoming Bruce or Johnny Cash. I want the crinkled skin and the scar on his hand when the tire iron slipped, and I want him to cradle those glass hearts and build a special mahogany carrying box for them. That's the silly princess hope of this girl, so I hold up Johnny Cash songs like paper cutouts, and I see what men fit inside, and then I kiss their necks or, worse, sit and understand.

"You sick little girl," say the shrinks.

"Come here, baby," say my men. "I'm sorry, I swear I'm gonna figure everything out."

LOVE AND INDUSTRY: A MIDWESTERN WORKBOOK

1.

Fall in love with a blue-faced sign for Interstate 35W in Minneapolis; ache and hold back tears because Minnesota winters are so cold and the sign has no choice but to shudder and brave the wind like a ragged prayer flag. This is the way you fall in love with viaducts, chipped concrete with steel veins of rebar, the way you fall in love with a telephone pole covered with rusted, industrial-strength staples, the posters for rock shows all melted away by weather and time. Whenever you are falling out of love, walk the alleys and find strange bits of metal from old machines and put them in your pockets, on tables and mantles.

2.

Believe in pivot points and fulcrums. Believe in the blank hole in the middle of a wrench, in the small spaces you swing around in order to change trajectories. Believe in a wad of chewed gum on a nice old wooden desk; the gum still has some of its pink, and that gives you hope. Believe in the solace of a streetscape when you are worried, slightly lost, happy, sad, caffeinated, tired, tinged with the sweetest of grays, tucked into a corner of a map.

3.

Look left as you drive across the concrete skin of an overpass girded with mud and weeds in Columbus, Ohio. Catch in a snapshot flash the glint of dulled metal and the ocean ripple of a blue plastic tarp, a 1970s-model van, and a lean-to propped up with sticks and a mop handle. Fear lives like Thoreau in his little cabin, with the sound of rushing water where the silty mud welcomed the first brave fishes ashore. Tell your children the fairy tale of the Billy Goats Gruff, growling to imitate the voice of the troll who waits under the wooden planks to snatch the littlest one. Envy the places where bridges are just bridges. Remember that if you are thrown out of the last rented room, the river's muddy and beaten arms will catch you.

4.

Feel the quiet of a burned-out steel mill on your skin. You shoot through Hammond, Indiana, heading for the bristling bouquet of Chicago's dark glass and metal. Turn your head to the corrugated leviathans that would never sneer at you. The long, slow mills have no choice but to accept the rust, the loss of fire and molten metal. The brown-black buildings, with the rows of windows up high like the portholes on a ship, let you love them in all their brokenness, with warehouses and parking lots that fade to gravel and crabgrass.

A concrete loading dock doesn't ask anything of you, doesn't demand that you agree with its crazy stories or its lies—and that is love, after all. It will wrap you in the baked-cookie smell of rain on warm asphalt and the earth's industrial rows of monocrop corn stretching on either side of the highway. It will give you billboard-sized abstract paintings in layers of faded paint and chipped brick and colors that haven't been named yet. You can read a philosophy on those surfaces, can vaguely make out the palimpsest of hope in the foreign language of a splash of yellow that somehow survived on those lovely, pockmarked metal walls.

5.

Look for industry in its purest form, pushing up its tender shoots after a forest fire, in places like Linden, a bombed-out neighborhood in Columbus razed by the war on drugs and racist zoning. The rows of boxy old houses once welcomed men home from World War II to a humming economic engine kick-started with ammunition, and now bullets rain like fireworks along streets with names like Bremen and Dresden, an echo of German destruction.

Count the side businesses. Cardboard signs on front lawns advertise Avon and childcare. A sign on a telephone pole reads, "Looking for Chemo Patients. Wigs, call 891-7633" and another, "Clothes for Concrete Geese." Sex workers lean into the windows of idling cars, negotiating, selling.

Wave every day to the neighbors who eat popsicles and sing along to classic rock in the sunshine as they wield their wire strippers, mining the scrap copper from spools of salvaged wire to sell to the metal yard. They might do crack occasionally, one man tells you, but they aren't crackheads. They called the cops to shut down a rival crack house on the next block.

Notice the two-by-four propping up the front porch roof of a house that leans slightly to the left. Learn to see it not as static trash but as a project in slow metamorphosis, a question, an option. Additions and rooms blur in awkward styles and shapes from the fronts and backs of houses like the new growth of leaves in a slightly brighter shade of green.

Listen—be aware of your judgment and push against it—as you stand next to the professional recycler who rides a modified bike he has made into a cart with a trailer and two garbage cans, complete with a full-sized boom box powered by a car battery. He has a grabber with a handle so he doesn't even have to get off the bike.

Watch the fear and awe and unnamed emotion in your gut as Crystal stops in front of you. She pushes two babies in two buggies, a lawnmower twisted with wire to the handles, pulling the mower as the buggies move in a rattling parade. Her husband doesn't want her to work. She asks if you need your grass cut. One baby keeps whipping his bottle into the street. She draws, too, shows you a unicorn she designed and had tattooed on her calf.

6.

See, and then do not see, what road you have chosen. The problem with your philosophy of industrial wreckage is that if you commit to loving and living in a warehouse or a ruined place, you launch a Superfund-scale, chain-link reclamation with dumpsters and barrels. The danger is similar to loving the punk rock boys, the weathered ones cradling their aching heads, with their beat-up Converse and their wily hair, their twitching, nicotine-stained fingers grabbing guitars, the boys smashing beer cans and singing songs that burn brighter when backlit with the supernova trail of impending collapse. What else is there to love?

ALL IN THE FAMILY

Like most kids of the seventies and early eighties, I was terrified about the threat of nuclear war. Unlike most kids, though, by age ten, I was as familiar with a Geiger counter as I was with a typewriter. So I considered myself lucky; in the event of a nuclear holocaust, I would know what to do. I knew about lead shielding, about iodine pills, about half-lives and decontamination.

My parents' business helps industries and hospitals around the country to use radiation safely and then to dispose of nuclear waste. My mother still runs the office end of things, and my father has driven all over the country, pulling a Geiger counter out of his car trunk as he has visited his clients on the road, making sure the nuclear medicine departments and industrial gauges in small towns across middle and southern America were running properly.

We traveled with him to hospitals throughout the South and Midwest. The test sources and gauges lived in the trunk, covered with formed lead semicircles and flexible lead shielding, soft as clay and inviting to the touch, but we were told to wash our hands afterward.

A career in the radiation field wasn't my father's lifelong dream. He wanted to go to medical school but couldn't afford it, as one story goes. His parents had emigrated from a farming community in Germany to Arkansas with nothing but their children in tow. My grandmother used a shotgun to destroy the rattlesnakes that slithered into the cabin they first lived in, a dugout in the soil.

After helping my grandfather butcher cows, my father worked in a geriatric ward, sold pots and pans door to door, and worked in a pill factory. He came north to Chicago, hoping for a construction job on the Sears Tower, which was then being built. He took correspondence courses in cartooning and trained as a locksmith. He became a highly intelligent scientist, a successful businessman with just the slightest trace of southern twang in certain words and a hell-bent work ethic. My mother emigrated from Germany, alone, when she was sixteen and found her way to the German-speaking community where my father grew up. After earning her GED, she took night courses in accounting and business management while working full time in my father's office and raising three kids. Through floods and computer hard drive meltdowns and coworker drama, she has served as the heart of the business and kept it running smoothly. She would never brag about jumping cultures and languages or learning accounting in her spare time, even when forced.

My parents worked hard. Radiation kept us fed, and for many years, the office was a wing of the house, and the business the primary topic of dinner conversation. As with most family businesses, we were all employees. When I was four or five, I stamped our return address onto envelopes and peeled apart the carbon-smelling sheets of colored invoices. From third grade through high school, I stapled together leak test kits—used to detect contamination—for a nickel apiece, and I put on a pot of coffee for the office in the morning before going to school. I learned to type there, and I eventually assembled reports detailing consultants' visits to various hospitals. As I got older, I answered phones, copied and collated endless radiation safety training manuals, cleaned the office on weekends, and filed during the summers. I remember the procession of secretaries and consultants like family members. They babysat us, we played with their kids, and we watched soap operas together in our living room during their lunch breaks. Work surrounded us, and we knew intimately its pitches and yaws.

———————

Over the years, as hospitals consolidated and the contracts went to larger corporations, the business has tended more and more to closing out abandoned sites where radiation was used. Now that my father is retired, the business has turned more toward "decon," a contract to decontaminate a large area, usually industrial, where a spill has occurred, where the clean-up staff has to wear protective suits that cover them from head to toe and that need to be changed regularly. They also get calls from the city of Chicago before anyone digs into the earth downtown to clear a foundation for a new building. They mind the mistakes of history, tracking trash and debris from the Great Chicago Fire a century and a half ago. After the fire, the rubble was spread along the shoreline so the city could rebuild, which deposited a layer of radioactivity from the factories that made lantern filaments.

I am proud that my family has done this dangerous and vital work, but I'm far removed from it, and they are a bit suspicious of the work I do at the keyboard. I think they might see me as another leaky barrel emitting dangerous traces from old stories. I understand the risks of attempting to shed light, and I would rather mark the places where the danger is buried.

———————

The names of the cities and the hospitals and factories we visited with my dad bring me a strange sort of nostalgia: Keokuk, Little Company of Mary, Cedar Rapids. With my mother's ingenuity, we entertained ourselves in hot hospital parking lots, air-conditioned hospital cafeterias, small-town gift shops, and parks. Toward the end of the day, we'd be so bored that we could only sit and stare at the hospital entrance, waiting for my father to emerge with his hard plastic briefcase in one hand and a survey meter in the other.

The scientific terms of radiation work—pica, rad, curies, millirem, dosimeter—arouse in me a pride at seeing my parents acting with confidence, knowing things and making decisions. I wonder now if this complete absorption with the office was only a product of financial need. Did we pull together because it takes a lot of teamwork for a small business to survive? Something tells me that there might not have been such an undertone of stress if we had been marketing pet food. But at least for me, the feeling of tension around the office, the sense of urgency, was intensified because of my fears about the power of radiation.

Like many children my age, I was brought to near-hysterics on a nightly basis, thinking about whether nuclear war would happen while I was sleeping. The prayer, "If I should die before I wake . . .," always seemed tinged with foreboding, as if I were tempting fate, so I barely ever said it. It's hard for me to know which came first: my morbid imagination or the cleanup training videos that seemed to play in an endless loop in our living room. The first short stories I wrote were all set on some sort of postapocalyptic desert landscape populated with genetically altered life-forms. The Cold War rhetoric on TV seemed to be condensed and stored in an office closet where radioactive sources were kept in round cement holes with heavy lids. When I asked my father about whether his work was dangerous, he consoled me with clipped sentences, graphs about exposure, and drawings that proved that sitting near a shielded source was safer than sitting too close to the television. When I asked about accidents and Three Mile Island, there was always a reassuring scientific answer to soothe my worry.

In *Nuclear Culture*, Paul Loeb describes a United Nuclear employee who explained to a fourth-grade class, "You know when you come home, kids, you're all dirty and your mother says you have to take off your shoes and sweatshirt? Well, nuclear safety is the same sort of thing."[1] In the same way, my father visited my fourth-grade class to talk about his job. He wanted to make radiation safety a part of our lives, and he passed out little party favors that the Nuclear Regulatory Commission must have produced, each a cardboard holder containing a black marble inside a clear plastic shell. The cardboard was printed with a nature scene and an explanation about how, in the future, our nuclear waste would all be stored safely in some kind of shielded, glass-like substance. Most of the kids had pulled the pellets out of their plastic coverings by the end of the school day. The marbles rolled across the scuffed linoleum during spelling class, lodged under the radiator, or waited to trip a stumbler with untied shoes. From about fifth grade onward, my main argument against the safety of nuclear power was that nobody, and no technology, is perfect.

We never lingered on the danger all around us. We focused on safety, on how meltdowns could be prevented, how safety mechanisms would kick into place. Loeb's description of Hanford, Washington, in *Nuclear Culture* could be a model

1 Paul Loeb, *Nuclear Culture*, New Society Publishers, 1987, p. 185.

for many towns across the US, a nuclear company town built to construct weapons and, later, the raw material for nuclear power. He described a city full of citizens who were both aware of corruption, error, and real danger at work and who could function through the power of denial.

Despite the abstract training materials, statistics, and marble euphemisms, reality became clearer during my sophomore year of high school, when a core meltdown at Chernobyl spewed fallout across Russia and Europe and into the world's jet stream. The contamination was classified as "low level" merely because the materials involved were not used to make a nuclear bomb. I began to pay more attention to my father's business and the industry's mistakes. I remember calls we received in the middle of the night about a spill: Could my father come right away or send some of his "guys" out in the morning? A truck had been leaking waste all over the road from St. Louis to Kentucky—an accident that would not appear on the evening news.

One of my jobs in the office around this time was to reorganize the library. The training brochures and medical journals I leafed through described routine accidents where unsuspecting people were contaminated and then suffered horrible radiation burns, cancer, and death. The brochures also included steps for treating these disasters. I read about the latest technology for soaking up liquid contaminant and the rate at which barrels began to leak when they were placed in the ground. I remember a colorful laminated booklet that depicted an apparently common scenario: a radioactive source is encased in shielding and becomes a gauge for use in a factory, maybe to check the level of soup in a can. The gauge is sent overseas. Years later, the equipment is dismantled, its function unknown, and poor children scavenging for food at the dump find the source and break it open to play with the brightly colored powder, thus contaminating themselves and an entire village.

I remember hearing about another poor community in central Illinois; a developer so badly wanted the profits from a waste dump in the town that he erased a water table on a geologic map of the area and submitted the altered documentation with his proposal. He hoped to get a piece of the nuclear promise, which had offered an endless supply of clean energy, enough to fuel an American lifestyle forever.

Maybe it was my worry about these stories that led me to send part of every one of my Pizza Hut paychecks to Greenpeace. I then went away to a private wannabe-Ivy in Minnesota, an overwhelming and challenging resocialization. Talking with students from Seattle and the Upper West Side, hearing about how other kids had grown up, what they liked to do, I learned about class difference. Standing among a group of freshmen at an ice-cream social or some other forced-bonding experience, someone asked, inevitably, what my folks did for a living. "Nuclear safety and nuclear waste," I answered. What I had expected in response was a reflection of my own feelings about the matter at that point: concern, questions about the problems related to waste disposal, comments on the raging debate about the proposed long-term storage site at Yucca Mountain in Nevada. Instead, there was a silence in which the other kids looked at each other. Then came the laughter.

"Like Homer Simpson!" someone crowed.

I had stunned them with something unique, I guess. The trick about "my father disposes of nuclear waste" became a party gag I yanked out for show-and-tell, a conversation starter. Now I wonder why it was funny, why even today my coworkers conversant in social justice theories about economic class and work stigma respond to this admission with wide eyes and giggles. Maybe the idea of actually disposing of waste somewhere in the Midwest fit with some people's vision of backwardness. None of the parents of my New York friends had jobs that placed them in bodily danger. Was nuclear waste some modern hyperbolic poop joke, a messy thing that nobody wanted to talk about?

I never thought too much about the ironic laughter, although I sent away for an application to the state school back home, thinking I might like to fade into the woodwork. But by that time, I'd discovered the campus environmental groups and become immersed in campaigns to fight toxic exposure and the exploitation of workers in that sleepy Minnesota town. When I helped organize protests against the "temporary" storage of nuclear waste on the floodplains of the Mississippi River, right across the road from the Prairie Island reservation of the Mdewakanton people north of Minneapolis, I learned about the nuclear industry from the outside in.

I began to read more about the links between nuclear power propaganda ("it's safe and economical and provides jobs") and nuclear arms propaganda ("it's safe and provides jobs and we have no choice"). I learned that there's a symbiotic relationship of sorts between nuclear plants and nuclear arms: a one-thousand-megawatt reactor produces five hundred pounds of plutonium per year. To make an atomic bomb, you need ten pounds of plutonium. I stuck a flashlight inside an empty plastic Twizzlers container to create a glowing "waste" barrel to use as a protest prop; it was meant to symbolize the ninety-two million gallons of liquid nuclear waste sitting in corroding, often leaking storage tanks. I asked my parents if they'd send me disposal safety gear to use in street theater. They declined. I felt guilty for going to college on money made from the nuclear industry, not really putting together that my family was involved in safety, that they were a tiny and ethical mom-and-pop shop in an industry involving massive players, payoffs, and global politics.

I learned about my parents being exposed to radiation while standing at a pay phone outside a sushi restaurant in the early summer of 1994. I'd moved to the East Coast after graduation, wanting to explore the country and get some distance. I had been working the overnight shift six days a week at a residential home for teenagers. I'd heard nothing from my mother for two weeks.

When I reached her at the office, her voice had an edge. I asked if she was OK, and she said she hadn't slept in a few nights. I asked her why, and she said that she and my father had been exposed. As in, exposed to radiation? I think I answered with a yell and a rapid fire of questions. I asked what it meant, and why she hadn't called.

"It's fine. We've just been really busy."

I was stunned that something this serious would happen and I would hear nothing about it. She described what had happened, and I asked her repeatedly, "Aren't you scared?"

She said, "We didn't have time to be scared."

A faulty monitoring device hadn't registered any contamination as my dad left a job site. He drove home in the pickup, came into the office, and walked around, touching carpeting, desks, files, and walls. My mother carried the survey meter in from the car and contaminated her hands and her desk. Then my dad went back to work to help recalibrate a survey meter. When he turned the meter on, it went crazy, clicking up in the high ranges. The first assumption was that the meter was broken or needed a new battery. When they removed it from my father's vicinity, the clicking slowed. The meter had been working fine, they realized, and the source was my dad.

My parents worked day and night to rip up the carpeting, test and retest the areas. They scrubbed their skin and were evaluated and monitored. They had to have someone haul away part of the seat of their pickup truck. State employees working for the Nuclear Regulatory Commission had to come in over the weekend to survey the office and supervise the disposal of everything that had been, as they say in the industry, "crapped up."

After hearing the news, I hung up and sat on the curb. I imagined my parents' deaths, even though my mother had said there weren't going to be any long-term effects. How could there not be? They had always assured me there was nothing to worry about.

Around that same time, I was editing a training manual about radiation safety for my mother, seeing the way that materials produced by government agencies attempt to downplay the risks of radiation. According to the statistics, drinking coffee will take six days off the average life expectancy. Working with nuclear waste will take off forty days, or so they say. So I assume you can either drink double espressos and eat an occasional hot fudge sundae or work in a reactor. And, as the guide says, "Nuclear industry ranks below mining, construction, agriculture, transportation, all industries, and government in number of deaths for 10,000 workers for 40 years." But I haven't ever heard of a farm having a core meltdown.

Later, I walked home dazed and called a close friend. There was concern in his voice, but I could tell that it wasn't something he could be empathetic about; it was too unreal. He mentioned the movie *Silkwood* and asked if my parents had to go through something like the decontamination scenes. I remembered seeing clips of the shower scene, the frantic portrayal of activist and whistleblower Karen Silkwood after she learned she was forty times over the legal limit.

Silkwood had been working at a Kerr-McGee nuclear plant. The company's name winds itself like DNA through my childhood. Silkwood was killed in a suspicious car accident. I have never watched the movie, despite being a labor activist, despite all the connections. I did not watch the series *Chernobyl* either. It is all too close, as if the glowing rods and core of my childhood, the money that powered my escape, my education, even my ability to sit here at this glowing screen, are still tightly wound together, still radiating their ghostly power.

CHICAGOLAND

Chicago is a dark jewel on the lake, an implacable garnet, a bristle of quartz towering next to a turquoise expanse. Its stones are set in a bezel ring of gray highway. A rough backdrop highlights the sparkle as further rings of gray asphalt reach outward, framing a semi-industrial backdrop called Chicagoland.

———————

To an outsider, the word "Chicagoland" might evoke a theme park where you can ride the Capone-a-Con or the Checker-Club Blues Experience, where you'd line up to buy an eight-dollar hot dog on a poppyseed roll with relish and a pickle and then hug a plush-costumed figure dressed like Jane Addams. If Chicagoland were a theme park, I would pay to visit, and then I would feel empty, wanting the ineffable that would be absent.

———————

I grew up in New Lenox, Illinois—twenty-four miles from the nearest edge of the Chicago city limits. To explain and locate New Lenox, I say, "It's far southwest of the city, right next to Joliet. You know: *Blues Brothers*, the prison," and people all around the world nod and say, "I've driven through there on I-80."

———————

Am I a suburban kid claiming affiliation with a city I only drove into for grade-school museum trips and supervised parental expeditions to buy Christmas chocolate at the old evergreen-colored Marshall Field's? Yes. Kind of. I am also someone who took high school drives up to see bands at the Cabaret Metro on Clark Street, who drove up to play indoor soccer and drove home on the cold highways alone, listening to Muddy Waters and Paul Butterfield on the radio, absorbing the blues, taking for granted that every city's nighttime airwaves would be soaked in such wailing ache. My friends and I drove downtown aimlessly, not having money to actually do anything and not knowing what to do, then drove home. I am someone who later took the commuter train to work, then still later moved into the city, crossing a divide and falling in love with the neighborhoods knit together by the elevated rail.

I am not from Chicago, but I am from Chicagoland. At first, I couldn't explain what I meant—I just *knew*.

Back when my husband, Cliff, was my boyfriend, he overheard me tell a stranger I was from Chicago. He scoffed at me in that gentle mocking I seem to invite from the world at large. *You're from corn, not Chicago,* he might have said.

"No," I replied, insistent, maybe rising from my seat to express something with a finger upheld, putting something into words that up until now might never have needed to be uttered: "No, I am actually from a place that is called . . . Chicagoland."

He joked with me: "I'm from about two hours east of Pittsburgh. Is that far East Chicago?"

"No!" I said. "There is no East Chicago. It's just the lake." Though within the far reaches of East Chicagoland is Gary, Indiana, which is somehow, inchoate in my mind, also Chicagoland.

He drew a rough map on a scrap piece of paper. I tried to sketch the boundaries, and he reached in with a pen to circle the entire Midwest.

It turns out we were both right.

———————

The friendly round-faced man with glasses and a blue work shirt who appeared on our Zenith television told me as a child that Empire Carpets served greater Chicagoland. Invisible ladies' voices sang a number—"588-2300: EMPIRE!"—that I remember even when I cannot remember the phone numbers from either of my childhood homes.

———————

Chicagoland was built by empire: violence, settlement, tentacles of transit, and waves of immigration crashing on the prairie's shore. The land had been a center for trade and transit for centuries before Europeans arrived, first a part of the Mound Builders' vast civilization centered downstate in Cahokia, then later the home of the Ojibwe, Odawa, Potawatomi, Miama, Ho-Chunk, Menominee, Sac, Fox, Kickapoo, and Illinois Nations. Indigenous peoples endured the seizure of land, forced relocation, illness, and murder, with not a single acre in the state set aside as reservation land, though they remain a vital presence in the city today.

The colonial instinct to rename as a way to christen and erase continued. Colonel Robert R. McCormick, publisher and editor of the *Chicago Tribune*, is said to have put the term "Chicagoland" into common usage in 1926 on the paper's front page: "Chicagoland's Shrines: A Tour of Discoveries." He gave this gritty kingdom a name and claimed that his land reached out two hundred miles in every direction to include parts of Wisconsin, Indiana, Michigan, and Iowa.

———

Today, the *Tribune* defines Chicagoland as the city itself plus all of Cook County, eight Illinois counties, including Will County where I grew up, and two counties across the line in Indiana. The Illinois Department of Tourism plucks Chicago out and describes Chicagoland as the remaining portion of Cook County plus the counties of Lake, DuPage, Kane, and Will. The Chicagoland Chamber of Commerce is inclusive: the city plus its ring of six adjoining counties. Today in Chicago, the term "Chicagoland" is a practical and unselfconscious term of internal reference. Businesses use it to denote their locations; phone companies, government agencies, and transit authorities use it to describe their coverage and service areas.

———

I don't know whether the north suburbs call themselves Chicagoland or whether they need to. I know they have distinct and glowing identities all on their own. You can say

"Evanston" and people know well enough: Northwestern University and a "beautiful town."

―――――――――

New Lenox, while nice in its own humble way, is not "beautiful." It's a former farm town in Will County that has aged like a cheap facelift in mildly horrific ways. We are an affordable bedroom community, and our face has frozen lumps of Botox McMansions studded in between the wrinkles of vinyl-sided older neighborhoods that used to be the only places to live. We are now the intersection of I-80 and the third beltway of I-375, the economical alternative.

―――――――――

To me, Chicagoland includes the unclaimed, non-notable spaces like these, where waves of European immigrants and Black migrants from the Great Migration settled as they moved out of downtown but somehow never escaped the city's grasp, never wanting to surrender their jewel. Chicago is not present without the liminal space you must cross to get to Chicago, and Chicago is not one of those snooty places that cares whether you are "in" or "out" according to a dividing line. Chicago is a bristling dominion that looks out across the corn and goofily, cheekily wants it all.

―――――――――

Chicagoland is a ruined beauty, the roadside that glitters with grit that edges the corn. It is the kingdom bounded by highways that have names instead of numbers: the Edens, Kingery, Lake Shore, the Dan Ryan, the Stevenson. We are the ends of all those roads. Chicagoland is Chicago's garage. We are the long, low, rusted warehouses where Chicago parks its snowplows and stores its extra couches. When Chicago takes off its coat, we hold it. We park its car.

Sometimes I say I am "from Illinois," but that feels as disingenuous as saying I am from "Chicago." I am not a rural kid by nature, nor am I urban. Nor am I from the suburbs, with their connotations of safe, contained experience. Chicagoland anchors the city like a rivet onto the Rust Belt. Joliet Township High School's mascot is still the Steelman, a bent and hulking figure made of welded metal panels. When Chicago turns fitfully in its sleep and remembers the steel and the stockyards, Chicagoland nods its head and holds those stories in its contaminated chain-link squares of earth.

Chicagoland is Svengoolie, a weird zombie-clown host on 1980s local network television who introduced old horror movies and whose signature joke was to simply intone, "Berwyn!" Berwyn is a nonremarkable town due west of the city: take Cermack out past Cicero, between the spokes of I-290 to the north and I-55 to the south. If you are from Chicagoland, you know that the drive out will be a stretch of strip malls and a mix of Mexican restaurants, Polish delis, Irish bars, fast-food places, nail salons, and auto parts stores.

Berwyn once featured a strange tall sculpture called *Spindle* by Dustin Shuler, which was a tall spike on which eight cars were impaled like bugs.

Spindle was featured in a drive-by scene in the Mike Myers movie *Wayne's World*, set in Aurora, another Chicagoland town still farther west in the same pie-slice between highways. Chicagoland is Wayne and Garth in an imaginary basement in Aurora, wanting to party even though they're heavy metal dorks in a paneled room, crying, "We're not worthy!"

Chicagoland is worthy in its secret ways, and it will take itself down a notch before you get the chance to. It is in the gleam in Wayne's eye and the pointed edge of *Spindle*, which was torn down to make way for a Walgreens. Chicagoland either is or is not Chicago itself, and Chicagoland doesn't need to know the answer to that question, because it loves Chicago like nobody else loves Chicago.

MILLER HIGH LIFE, THE CHAMPAGNE OF BEERS

The rich smell of nicotine on fingertips reminds me of a home-knitted afghan. The *pssst* of a beer can or the clink of ice in a glass sound like the wind chimes and breezes of home. I have loved men for their intelligent hands—the rough and scarred ones that remind me of my uncle and my grandfather—rimmed in grease or calluses. I was happy for those hands when I saw them lift something as light as an aluminum can or perform a gesture as automatic as the gentle thumb-flick on the end of a cigarette.

I even love the warm barn-smell of a cold unlit cigarette, neat in its silver paper like a chocolate, so much that I cannot touch them anymore. If I could, I would rather smoke salads than eat them. I know the midwestern winter afternoon burr of leaf-burning char, the warm sweater-weather shouldering into liquid fire. I know the taste of spiced cut-grass honey. I know the first inhale of a cigarette, which tastes best in slight precipitation and cold when I'm standing on a bridge over a river or creek. I know the exhale, where it balloons windless and diffuse in front of you like an idea you can't quite remember. I know the exhale into the wind where it is ripped from your mouth like a sail or a scream.

Before any other brain-changing substance, my bedrock was carved by trickling underground streams of Miller High Life. The golden cans lay like logs in the vegetable drawer of the fridge until I received my call: *Getmeabeerwouldya?* I hefted open the fridge door, feeling so strong at four and five. The cans rattled as I pulled at the drawer's plastic handle.

Near the tops of the bottles and cans was printed the image of the Miller lady, sitting in the hitch of the moon's curve. She smiled, surrounded by stars, and wore a red, striped dress and a flower in her hair. She was what the Morton salt girl got to be when she grew up and went to heaven for a party.

On special good-mood nights, I got to use my own beer mug, a tiny amber glass shaped like a barrel. I sipped and wrinkled my nose at the bubbles. The earthy foam seemed to have emerged from a spring's crevice. Its texture reminded me of bath bubbles or whipped cream on a sundae. The beer itself smelled like freshly cut two-by-fours of pine, or maybe old books. They said it was an adult taste, like my mother's pickled herring or my father's tinned sardines. Your tastes will change, they said. Adults seem drawn toward the metallic and the earthen, the bitter, on their way to death and the earth's embrace.

On my tongue, High Life had a smooth warmth, an almost playful bite like a puppy's snap. It didn't growl or threaten like flat drinks called "on-the-rocks," which sounded like shipwrecks waiting to happen. The taste of Miller High Life is all mixed up for me with the easy nap of our old golden velour couch, smushed and comfortable and only alive in my memory, my father's hairy forearms draped over the armrests of the matching gold chair.

The first beer was the best beer. When they started to stack up, when the cans were crushed into irregular disks like cartoon car-accident victims, Dad went away from the tension and into sleepy and gone. That first beer: that golden window. I was the one who got to deliver relief, to make it better. That's the illusion I labored under, part of the larger expectation of myself to soak up the pain of others.

It's hard to explain how a child senses the flavor of a parent's pain. I knew then—or would know later, within a few years—that my father had come from a kind of tornado himself and that he was still spinning.

The slick aluminum cans of High Life in the pale turquoise crisper drawer must have looked, in the 1970s, like the future. We loved to watch *Space: 1999*, a show about deep space exploration in ships shaped like segmented aluminum cans. We loved to imagine airless colonies and warp speed. It's amazing how the future can be such a solace because of its blankness and its promise of something new somewhere far away on a different planet. In television's serialized low-budget space, there seemed to be no bars, no baggage, no debt, no poverty, and no families. The future looked like aluminum cans, like our angular fridge—no need to defrost!—and like the modern sight of a no-iron, cotton-poly V-necked T-shirt. When I got to taste Miller High Life, I was overjoyed because I was included, because we were playing, because we were laughing, because he was laughing. We were drinking the future.

Miller comes in a classic form: Miller High Life, with a logo that's shaped like a white puffy bowtie outlined in red. Miller also makes MGD—Miller Genuine Draft—a brand betrayal that I feel irrationally disgusted by, as severely flawed as episodes one through three of George Lucas's *Star Wars*. Like a fervent nationalist defending a tiny, corrupt homeland, I hate MGD as a bastardization of High Life. Maybe I am angry at MGD because it stands for the slick and cold marketing of the eighties, a decade when I began to consider its impact on my life.

Miller High Life has a slogan on its bottles and cans: "The Champagne of Beers." This is so earnest and hopeful it becomes unintentionally funny, like calling a Ford Fiesta "The Rolls Royce of Economy Cars" or Bacos "The Filet Mignon of Processed Meats." The tagline tips its hand a bit too much in its eagerness to include one group with another, the working and lower-middle class in with those who enjoy a truly comfortable life of leisure. Half of its promise is entrance: drink this to grow larger and to solve class struggle with one relaxing sip.

The slogan, so simple, contains a subtle deconstruction, an edge. It's similar to the way "happy hour" at a bar voices a truth: we've come from work where we were not happy at all. It's freeing to have the class divisions distilled in a slogan that is a quarter-joke: sure, buddy, you can have the high life in a can. Nobody's that stupid. We don't get champagne. But we don't want it anyway. We like our beer just fine.

Behind the slogan's goofiness, and then behind its edge, is a sliver of sweet hope; the high life might be a blissful plane, the promised land, the place where you go when you've made it and nothing can touch you. It technically doesn't make any sense: The beer itself (High Life) modifies this essence (high life) as if the high life were made by Miller, as if Miller were the portal. At the same time, the high life remains completely undefined, so you might be sitting in it right now. It invites you to define this paradise, to step into it: the high life of the upper classes, the life that's so sweet because you're finally high and nothing can touch you. It offers the ultimate promise that inside this beer is not a temporary buzz, disappointing and irritating when it fades to a headache. Instead, this beer is a new life, as if it might allow one to be born again on a higher level of existence.

When my dad sat in his chair to drink his beer in the dark living room—the flicker of the television casting blue ghosts—what I saw on his face was the utter exhaustion of work. I saw purple smudges under his eyes and sallow skin, a rumpled white button-down shirt, and a shoulder slump. He and my mom were made of work; she would be working before we got up, and she would start again after we went to bed. My father was often on the road, and at the end of those trips, he would lug in his huge rectangular plastic briefcase and drop it in the hallway, where it would clatter on the tiles.

In this photo of my father, with my grandfather, Papa, in overalls, I see two men at different stages in their working lives. Papa's arms hang from crooked elbows. His arms are bent because they rest at readiness and have been frozen there; their natural state is motion. He is duck-footed from hauling and pushing and scrabbling for purchase against the earth. He looks small next to my dad but iron-postured. He, a German immigrant of the Old World, scarred by service in World War I and want and chaos in Germany afterward, never learned to smile in photos and was slow to show affection. From the space between their bodies, I see that my father's arm around his father's shoulder is not reciprocated. Papa's arms just hang there. He looks as though he could stand there staring for all eternity. That's how he always looked to me.

On my father's face, I see the relief of stepping away from butchering to get into medicine. He'd first helped slit open a cow when he was eight and hated it. These pictures of Dad, so proud in scrubs, always twist in my gut, because the door to medical school would soon be closed to him: it was too expensive, and there were other roadblocks. Medical school was where my father was meant to be, the route to the work he wanted but did not get.

As a child, I encountered a changeable father, one who could roughhouse and twist his face into a pirate grimace to make us kids squeal. Other times, I picked up my dad's tension and moods like a piece of tinfoil dented with the slightest touch. I reflected every wince and furrowed brow on my silver skin. He was that way, too, I think: the sensitive child of a changeable, moody man.

In creative writing workshops, I ask my students to read aloud a magical passage from James Agee's *Let Us Now Praise Famous Men*, a book that describes the lives of sharecroppers in Alabama in the 1930s. The passage simply describes a pair of overalls, colored as "a scale of blues, subtle, delicious, and deft beyond what I have seen elsewhere approached except in rare skies, the smoky light some days are filmed with, and some of the blues of Cézanne." Agee ends this careful praise song by describing worn, patched work shirts as "the feather mantle of a Toltec prince." When the students read the words aloud, I cannot help but mouth along to the rhythm as if it were scripture. It is not because I romanticize the imprint of hard work. It is because of the accuracy and the appropriateness of Agee's reverence.

———————

Maybe his meanness came from eating weeds in the Black Forest when there was no food, from fighting in World War I, and from losing everything in the German currency crash before World War II.

Papa did have a hard life, after all—harder than I can possibly imagine. Some of the ravages of work are written on men's bodies with their testosterone-layered muscles and their upper body strength. Work and class shape the man who works with his body, and pain carves its cruel blade into the man whose body is injured but keeps on working.

If someone would have explained, "We feel protective of him because he got royally screwed over at work," maybe I would have feared him less.

No one gave me the real story. Instead, I could only look inward, toward my instinct of shrinking back in fear, and read that as a sin. My fear was not only for the men with hard lives but also the fear for the work they did, for the way it would destroy them, and for the anger it sowed.

———————

Norman Lear's *All in the Family* debuted the month I was born—January 1971—and I came to consciousness amid the wavering happy strains of the theme song, "Those Were the Days," which expresses or parodies nostalgia for a time when "girls were girls and men were men."

Edith's flowered housedresses and fluttering hands and "Oh, Archie!" are imprinted in my brain like the gestures of my own family. And in my memory of Archie Bunker, there is always the can of beer. At the end of the workday, Archie came home to sit in his brownish-yellow armchair. He lifted a cigar and a can of beer to his mouth to soften the irritations of the world.

Archie was a bigot—a useful 1970s word—and Carroll O'Connor tricked me into loving this guy. But why? What was the meaning of this fueling station, this armchair, and this beer? I have a little yellow-armchair pocket of love in my heart for Archie. It turns out that he was not a drunk at all, even though the thing my child-brain remembered about him was his beer.

Archie's beer itself, on film, is a yellow can with red-and-black lettering that spells "Best Quality BEER," along with a slogan, "The Favorite Everywhere," and an ornate red lion logo connoting the Eastern European origins of many Rust Belt immigrant families who came to this country looking for work in the mines and later in steel.

I did not know that I lived in this swath of industry called the Rust Belt until I left and heard that sad name. Rust: as if there's nothing left but a fine brown filigree that crumbles like dirt in your hand. I knew I loved the look of a corrugated warehouse, of a whole run of them, and that a maze of lightly neglected patchwork small-shop industry smelled and looked like home. I think I loved Archie Bunker because of his voice, his beaten-down, home-from-work, forward slump of the shoulders, and his can of beer.

I don't know if other people loved Archie because they thought the Rust Belt roughness of his humble living room was ridiculous and narrow. I loved it because it looked and sounded like the places I knew.

By the time I was three or four, I knew you weren't supposed to call someone "Meathead," but the show's brilliance lay in balancing these fractious moments with affection. The underlying message I remember was that it was OK to yell and for women to yell back. When Archie bumbled into racism, the various flinches and eye-rolls of the supporting characters, the women, showed me more clearly than a grade-school filmstrip how wrong Archie was.

Archie Bunker didn't work in steel. His day's work was at the loading dock, driving a taxi, or cleaning as a janitor. I have loved Archie Bunkers and hated what work—the structured sadism of management, the chronic demand to prove yourself, the essential instability of a job today and none tomorrow—did to people I loved. In some cases, I put up with too much bullshit from partners because I sympathized with the pain of their nine-to-fives or seven-to-sixes or three-to-twelves. I wanted to be the ever-smiling Edith, but I was not sitcom material.

Still, as I pull apart the threads of drugs and drink in my life, I find them knotted at the root of work and its often arbitrary and intermittent cruelty. My sympathies for working men led me to pour out my patience in excess. I was caught in the fundamental mystery of modern life, where a man pours alcohol or powders or pills into the gears that might crush him.

"Happiness is primarily a matter of work that is fulfilling," says Buddhist writer Robert Aitken. Even if a person has family, hobbies, community, and more, Aitken writes, "if the job is unsatisfactory, nothing else can really compensate."

I have found this to be true in my own life. There have been times in my past in which I have wished for a subway crash to break my leg so I'd get time away from a job. There have been other times where my anxiety over the workday's drama bled into the minutes of my evening and my dreams. Sometimes, I felt I should have been paid for sleeping because my dreams processed the workday stress, wiping the slate clean for another day.

I knew work could suck. It didn't have to, not at all; it could sing with flow and the skill of dishes slung in a bus tub, of laughter across the kitchen, of the rush of hours and papers and tasks completed. Because flow and fun were possible, work was even more painful when it turned awful. And a boss could, with the tiniest of decisions, wreck your whole eight-hour life. Or maybe it was the boss above them who decided to save money and crank it up a notch. We were the notches. And we all had to suffer.

Most of my family had anxiety problems that came from the mental strain of various inhumane jobs and the stress of economic instability. I saw how work disfigured and devoured. I heard stories of hard work, and later, I would work long and hard with my own body and hands. I had seen my grandfather's finger stubs, the tops of two fingers severed in a meat grinder during his work at the Catholic abbey up the hill from his house. I was already a dedicated labor activist when I learned that the church fired him after it had taken its inches of flesh in sacrifice, because what good is an eight-fingered butcher?

Archie Bunker's entrance to his living room often came with a moan. He shuffled in and smashed his hat on the stand, exhausted. He made real that secret truth.

I was on Archie's side. I would keep his secrets. I would make of myself a poultice for his wounds.

_____

Carroll O'Connor, who played Archie, called *All in the Family* satire. The racism, sexism, and homophobia cast in sharp relief the ridiculousness of Archie's beliefs, but the show would not have been so beloved if Archie were a target of hatred and ridicule. For the show to connect with its viewers, they had to love him. And I did.

Archie worked hard, yet he was not beaten by work or life. He never puked on the floor or crossed the line into cruelty with Edith. Not trusting my memory, I watched old episodes to see him wavering back and forth between affection and irritability. Archie got flustered and slapped like a stooge against his affection and doubt, but his big heart rose up occasionally against his big mouth. He said what he thought, he scowled, and he shook his head, but he did not descend into an alcohol-fueled tirade of abuse. He served as a mouthpiece for a certain element of American culture, and other elements got to shout it out with him, back and forth, and everyone could laugh with the slightly nervous shock of the taboo out there in the living room, someone else's living room in an electric box inside our own.

_____

If work is horrible, one argument goes, you can at least take back control by numbing yourself to oblivion, either during or after your shift. I understand, in some way, the urge to numb oneself through work: a drink at lunchtime, a toke in the morning.

A man I loved confessed to me, during one phase in which he tried to get clean, that he smoked far more pot than I ever knew, that for just about every waking hour in which I saw his face, he was high. It was "wake and bake" every single day, he said. Work sucked, he said, and this was a way to get through it. The smell dissipated, and the red eyes were cleared with Visine.

Drugs or drink can easily become a personal religion. Like the most twisted forms of belief, the moments of ecstasy are spaced far and wide between the days of monotony, and attaining ecstasy requires single-minded devotion, obedience, and maybe even disdain toward the uninitiated. If all you have is chemical relief at the end of the day, the chemicals can make you cruel because the escape is so temporary, so disappointing. Your head and your home may become as much a living hell as your job, with no real escape.

———————

Karl Marx famously described religion as "the opium of the people," and most people see this as a simple dismissal. Later in the same paragraph, though, Marx also calls religion the "sigh of the oppressed creature." If religion equals opium and also equals the sigh of oppression, then opium also equals a sigh, an understandable movement toward blind comfort in a cruel world.

Opium, a derivative of the poppy, was huge in Britain in Marx's day. Prohibition groups sprang up, protesting British companies that profited off the colonial web and the international opium trade in Asia. Britain controlled the nation of Burma, brought opium into that Buddhist country, and built a supply chain to profit from the delivery of the drug between 1826 and 1948. The jails in Burmese provinces filled with opium addicts. When Marx wrote the word "opium," he was referencing a supply chain that numbed and generated profit, and maybe also one that numbed the worker.[1] British colonial officers might have liked opium for the same reasons. They wove chemicals and racism into an insidious system of control and profit. They believed that native Burmese got addicted but that Chinese immigrant miners and laborers supposedly became more productive on opium, that the drug helped them relax after work and allowed them to arrive ready for even more crushing work the next day.

If you're high, you have very little brainpower left to foment rebellion with others; this was one of the reasons temperance was a key tenet in European socialist movements in the late 1800s. In Marx's day, the temperance movement in Britain emerged as part of a larger sea change in culture that produced an awareness of the importance of childhood and child protection, rights for prisoners and the mentally ill, and democratic values. In other words, a focus on human rights emerged with the realization that substance abuse also affects families and children.

For me, substance abuse itself never stands alone. It is always tied to money and therefore to work, and sometimes, a role in the drug trade is the only industry available. If chemicals swallow a wage-earner, who will feed the children? A family can disintegrate like a slight fizzle of carbonation on the surface of amber beer, like whorls of smoke.

---

1 In the Burmese province of Arakan in 1869, up to half of adult males ages seventeen to thirty-five consumed opium. By the 1870s, the jails had filled with opium users. Local residents put together a petition to the British government to restrict opium sales. Ashley Wright, "Opium in British Burma, 1826–1881," *Contemporary Drug Problems* 35, Winter 2008, 611–646.

My mom tells me I turned "bad" when I was eight, within a year of Papa's death. I wasn't a bad child, like an egg gone rotten. I challenged her later on her word choice.

"Mom," I asked, "What do you mean, 'bad?'"

She clarified: "No, I don't mean bad. I mean angry. Sad."

It wasn't because I missed my grandfather. Our family's ship also seemed to tank when I was eight, in 1979, launching what my mom calls "the bad decade" for us. Two of my dad's employees quit, taking his files and contracts and setting up a rival business. Work was always there and never far away, like the rough metal trim that separated the bright red shag carpeting of our living room from the low, industrial-grade nap of the office hallway.

I remember my mom's cigarette always burning in the ashtray on her desk, and Dad's chain-smoking and evening six-packs. I remember his hollow-eyed look, his grayed skin, our perpetual sense of trying not to be noisy, of trying not to cause further stress, a sense that we could never suck enough stress out of the air. To make him feel better during one dire moment, I made him a rough card out of perforated dot-matrix printer paper. I pried the lid off a square tin decorated in hearts and flowers, where I kept my sticker collection, and I used all my best stickers, even the ones I could not bear to part with. I stuck green shiny dragons onto the card, hoping magically that with my sacrifice, if I gave more than I wanted to, I could make lasting happiness.

When I was eight, we did not want for anything material, but our bodies were messes from stress, each of us marked: headaches, stomachaches, hospitalizations, prematurely grayed hair, flaring arthritis, heart trouble, and panic.

My father and mother made heroic efforts to save the business and our family. They stayed together. My dad took a second job and worked there until I was in college.

———————

Now, I know eight from the outside. My son was eight when I first began writing this essay. I have seen us through a year of eight, and I can't see how badness or even sadness might emerge from a child's biology. I've also seen and known a number of eight-year-old girls, and badness does not seem to be part of their inherent nature. Stickers and glitter and shrieks, but not badness. I can only surmise that the badness my mother sensed in me had to come from the outside, a manifestation of stress or fear.

———————

In episode 137 of *All in the Family*, "The Unemployment Story," Archie comes in and grabs up his grandson, Joey, from the playpen in the living room. He snuggles him on his lap and tells him, "I hope you never had a day like I had today. Work thirty years for the same company and what do you get?" He delivers a raspberry.

He yells upstairs that he needs to talk to Edith. They exchange banter, and she groans down at him. Finally, he yells, "I got canned today. Fired, fired, fired!"

Edith comes down. She hugs him and pats his face, and he calmly lets her. There's no hint of yelling, and Archie does not use the fear of financial collapse to grab a beer and hunch darkly in his doom.

Instead, Michael ("Meathead") and Gloria arrive for a dinner to celebrate the sale of Michael's first article. Gloria crows that Michael is on his way to a lifetime of security. Archie says, "I wish they'd give that to people who really work for a living."

The beauty I didn't remember but must have swallowed gladly as a child was how consistent Gloria is in arguing with her father. As he grouses because he doesn't want to sing a song she wrote, she stands behind him and keeps swatting him on the head.

Finally, the news about the layoff comes out. Gloria stops and whispers, "I didn't mean to hurt you," and Archie replies, "I know you didn't."

That back-and-forth, the workingman who can talk feelings, gives me goosebumps and brings tears of longing to my eyes.

They all gather around Archie's chair, and Archie launches into a list of work-related malapropisms: "I'm a guy who always has his nose to the brimstone."

Gloria sits on his lap and kisses him, and the camera zooms in on his face, thoughtful and quiet.

I realize that Archie Bunker gave the child-me both a fantasy and an ideal. After living through partners who got canned and then came home to rage in an apocalypse of depression and hopelessness—and somehow blamed me because I didn't have to do that kind of work—I see more clearly the beauty of this moment, a fictional gathering together, a circling of the wagons in gentle human contact.

Archie might have had a beer with dinner that night, but no episodes showed his unemployment as a slide into depression that came with more crumpled empty cans, an unshaved face, or his form slouched in a chair for days. He got up the next morning, put on his plaid coat, filed for unemployment, and then started looking for work.

———————————

As a teenager, I scowled at my dad, pursing my lips over a mouthful of silver braces he'd paid for. He poured himself another cup of coffee so he could get to a job that wrote its stress in his body, but he pushed himself through it to keep a roof over our heads. My father and I are similar in temperament: analytic, perfectionist, anxious, stubborn, strong-willed. I saw him large and blurry on the horizon, standing in front of other stories I couldn't see: stories of work so hard it could drive you insane, economic instability, anxiety, the working class struggling to become middle class, the father, all fathers, all authority, drink, anger, all men. What happened was that, through an accident of time, I happened to be exposed to a transformative and rough few decades of his life. I suppose he would admit that, too, or maybe not.

Time wasn't what healed wounds. Time would have eased them over with layers of silt to bury them, which would have softened the edges a bit but still left the shapes to haunt my terrain. Instead, I went out into the world with that father-ache, the ache for a missing man with rough edges, and the world simply could not polish those rough edges quickly enough. And then I worked very hard to unearth, to reorient, to reconfigure my landscape.

Now he tells me how proud he is of me. He's a changed man: calmer, affectionate, and more thoughtful. Today, I claim from him my prodding intelligence, a skepticism and a rebellious streak that form the core of who I am. I see now that we are both on the same side. I am blessed with his brain, his olive skin, his wry laughter, his toughness, his messed-up feet, his crooked nose, and his skepticism. I would not be myself without him. Today, he has morphed from a heart attack sufferer into a relaxation guru watching webinars on meditation and taking classes in Tai Chi. He checks in, recommends vitamins, praises my writing in careful yet effusive words. This is not a diatribe but a testament to love through hard times. I don't take any of this new dad for granted, but he has shown me through the geography of his life that change is possible.

THE THIRD EYE OF
THE OYSTER

The engine inside me has rattled with anxiety since I was eight or nine, and I coaxed it down to a slow burn most days with an hour of walking. I walked alone, in the rain, in the wind, fists punched into pockets that made earthward points poking from the lining of my windbreaker. I was a walker in grade school and junior high, even though, where I grew up in northeast Illinois, there were no forests or bluffs or scenic hills. I liked to walk from our house to Haines School, where I had attended fourth grade, ten minutes on foot. In the summer heat after a rain, a fog rose up from the hot pavement into the cool air. I laid down on the blacktop. The warmth of baked tar spread along my legs, back, and arms, and I imagined I was floating. I walked for two miles in a loop, up and back, through our small town. In any direction, you could walk ten or fifteen minutes and be out into the corn grid, with the impenetrable blankness of those flat shiny leaves in every direction. It was not wild but still alien, an army of stalks in rank and file going nowhere.

Wildness was in the ditches, filled with chicory and daylilies and gravel and cattails, wrappers and shoes and smashed car parts—all clues to other lives. It would become my life habit: weird walks in city or country, along the backsides of warehouses and sad main streets with bankrupt cafes and bakeries where flies buzzed around the cookies in the display case, on long deserted roads, always courting danger. I thought it was a twisted, secret vice. I would have been delighted then to have known about Virginia Woolf, to have read her essay "Street Haunting," and to have heard her description of a cleansing walk to break "the shell-like covering which our souls have excreted to house themselves . . . and there is left of all these wrinkles and roughness a central oyster of perceptiveness, an enormous eye." I treasured the flashes of freedom in the eye of the storm.

In junior high, I walked in the rain, crying over the brimming teenage feeling of being constantly overwhelmed by the ambiguity ahead. I remember wearing my mother's blue-and-beige reversible raincoat. I remember a moment walking up a wet hill, slipping into a ditch with soaked shoes, and feeling so blissfully and sadly apart from the rest of the world.

In my late teens, I set out on a walk to the mall, which Google Maps now tells me is ten miles from my parents' house. I already had a driver's license, and I could have driven, but I wanted to see what it was like to get there on foot. It was weird and beautiful to see the gravel ribbons on the roadsides unroll so slowly. It was amazing to feel the sudden traffic blurt by in a rush of wind and then disappear, knowing I would still be on this road for hours. Maybe walking gives me the illusion of a different kind of progress. It let me know, in ghostly outline, a place whose previous lives, whose centuries of residents, had been scrubbed out, erased.

At twelve, an older guy from my school, casually astride a bicycle in a friend's driveway, reached a hairy arm over, pulled out the fabric of my T-shirt, and commented on what was growing inside. I just froze in a puff-faced half-smile, eyes narrowed but mouth turned up in an anxious grimace, not sure how to react, in a circle of guffaws.

"I'm going to rape you," said another boy as he trapped me in a cinder block stairwell of a hotel when I was eleven or twelve. Soccer and playing war with neighborhood boys in the construction sites behind our house had made me scrappy and strong, but I pushed against him and felt the bones in his arms locked around me. He was stronger. I hurt myself getting away, twisting and bruising, a burst that left me sweaty as I lunged for the door's curved metal handle.

What stands out now, excavating this kernel, is how I folded it inward. I tucked the moment away, like a chicken pecks a piece of gravel and stores it in the gizzard to aid with digestion. I knew about gizzards because Dad explained them once as we sat in a fried chicken restaurant, him eating from a bag of fried gizzards and reaching up to pick a piece of gravel from between his teeth. I was tough, the daughter of a tough and hardworking man, the granddaughter of impossible stories of survival. So I didn't tell my parents about something that small. Being trapped in a stairwell for a few moments: so what? So what—when so much worse had happened to them.

I had major events with men, to be sure, the traumas of having a man not stop when I said no, but here, I am interested in the constant background radiation, the cumulative effect of the daily tiny blows in a vulnerable person's life, in any life that doesn't conform. I think moments such as these—occurring at random in a flurry of confusion over years—sanded away my girlhood bravery like steel wool. I think, eventually, that bravery was replaced with something even tougher, but I admit that I am a little edgy and jumpy, more adult and wary than is helpful. When a ball on a pool table is buffeted equally from all sides, it stays in place, as if it has never been touched at all.

———————

That adventurous walk to the mall across the cornfields in my teens ended with a pickup truck that slowed as the driver leered out the window. I craned my neck both ways along the empty highway as the truck did a lazy U-turn and pulled up across the shoulder of the road, blocking my path. I picked up a large rock, sweaty and raging and exhausted, and screamed, "I'll break your windshield!" He laughed and accelerated away.

I never see that walk as a failure; I found a scrap of the American flag I made into a bit of art, and I found some pretty rocks. I loved to stuff my pockets with treasures. I found a red flannel shirt with snaps, and I took it home, washed it, and wore it proudly.

After the pickup truck, I was too concerned and bitten by adrenaline to cry. I flagged down a beat-up truck driven by an older, white-bearded farmer and gratefully accepted a ride back into town. I told no one. I thought then that my weirdness was my responsibility. What creature, ever, wants to range the roadsides and scrap-pick? Certainly not a *woman*. I had no idea about Woolf's "vast republican army of anonymous trampers." The danger was therefore all my fault. Now I see what a journeyer I was in a constrained land. I had gone through one year of college by then, been on my first hikes with an REI-equipped new set of friends, and I tried to apply those new lessons to my life in the corn grid.

A decade later, I was exhausted with my edge-wandering, and I had raised myself as an adult comfortable with the edges

Sonya Huber

and the undersides. That comfort is often a benefit, a third eye, but it can be a burden as a compass. I wanted someone rough enough to punch down faces and walls for me. I wanted to choose the path of least resistance. Such paths are never marked; I learned that a path can start easy, offering a false promise of an painless ascent.

In my twenties and thirties, I strung days together with the thread of an asphalt path near a river in Columbus, Ohio. I had to tire myself out like a gerbil on a wheel. I set a destination: a bridge or a bend in the path near the marsh. I folded my walk in half at that point and returned to where I started.

I mostly avoided the eyes of people who walked past, but I enjoyed the fact that I was not alone. Strangers passed me from behind or walked toward me from the opposite direction—sweaty runners; racing bikers with their heads down, barking, "on your left!"; strolling elderly women in thick-soled athletic shoes; people being pulled along by eager dogs. We moved together beneath the layered humid sky, beside the river strafed with sewage runoff after a heavy rain. We walked together amid the twigs, the curls of dried vines, and the nests of thistles and weed stalks, beneath the green fans of maple, amid the diagonal drifts of cottonwood fuzz, next to patches of mowed grass that seemed arid and sad like lined paper with nothing to be written on it. Much of the Midwest is written over twice or thrice, land stolen and farmed and carved and shaped, so a nature walk in a city always brings up ideas of damage wrought by humans and the question of coexistence without destruction.

Each day, I burst from the claustrophobia of my apartment, carrying an unsolvable future, a job search, or another frustration, and the first part of the walk would give me the release of flight and escape. I churned my feet, and sometimes I cried as I walked. When I came to my turning point, the apex of the walk felt for a moment like giving up and retreating, and I would slow and turn around, retracing my steps. Then the life I'd fled would reknit around me as I faced homeward, and return would feel like a small success, even though I had merely completed the ritual of stepping away and stepping back, bisecting an hour and then joining the halves. The light was bluer at my farthest point away, facing home. I tricked myself with the top of the walk, with the absence that made the heart grow fond, into wanting to be back there. I had held my life at arm's length for an hour before cell phones. No one could reach me, and I took regular scoops of virtue from the fact that I could stand to be alone that long.

The river water was brown, and under the bridge, the rocks were studded with turtles. Girls were raped and attacked along that path, and someone had hung themselves from a tree down near the school. The path was like walking along a lick of gnat-flecked sadness, as if I had to acknowledge my compulsion to walk in spite of the danger, nodding at the homeless men who sometimes camped up high beneath the concrete viaduct. Sometimes a flood receded and left a broad mulch of smoothed mud, which was then lined and tracked with bird prints and imprints of stems and leaves and bugs.

One time, a young man on a bike told me to come with him into the woods, and I said no. He got angry with me for refusing and stopped his bike on the bridge in front of me to block me from leaving, the same move the pickup truck had made years before. I breathed raggedly and sprinted around him and up the path. I ran toward a couple, wild-eyed and panting. I told them what had happened and then kept running. I still feel the moment like a metallic imprint, a sharp bas-relief in which I could easily have been no more.

If I am honest, I can say it has been hard for me to be alone. Even a narrow, pinch-faced girl like me has encountered so many strangers in parks, on streets, and on trains who offered a constant assault on the senses and broke my personal peace. On the steps of churches and standing in bars, I lied to the men who hit on me, always telling them I was married. I told them retro scenarios: *My boyfriend won't like it if I give you my number.* I didn't pull an aluminum bat from my trunk. I smiled to diffuse the conflict: *See, I'm not a bitch.*

The path led me to one man and another. I chose them partly for the relief of a pair of fists, so that I could fit into a place the world could understand. I chose someone who wanted to beat the shit out of anyone who would hurt me. I needed the specter of the imaginary man—and then real men who might love me enough to help me beat other men to a pulp if I were crossed, who might arrive any second in a jealous rage. I see it as understandable, given the constant needling hands stretching toward my body in strange cities alone.

Twilight fell with a yellow-orange block of shining sky above, a bristle of shadowed weeds below, and I saw what Woolf saw: "Passing, glimpsing, everything seems accidentally but miraculously sprinkled with beauty." She'd gone out to buy a pencil, her errand an excuse for the real purpose of filling and overfilling the storehouse of the soul. Life, too, paid me back a thousand times for every wrong with the baubles it cast on its shores for me to find.

A warehouse or garage hunkered beyond clusters of trees, part of a large center for developmentally disabled adults, complete with quiet parking lots and dark windows. This river path was nature's narrow spine, edged with the peaks of houses and crusted on both sides with the highway's rush. I could have loved a different path, lost myself somewhere farther in green and wild, but this was easy, nearby, and what I knew. I liked the strange hassle of human traffic, the preteen boys hunched like commas on their BMX bikes, hats askew. I liked to be reminded, I guess, that at any hour of the day, there were people seeking shelter under branches but that they too were finding only imperfect, thin relief.

The occasional biker whipped by, chain clanking, the ticking of the gears like the evening crickets. The marsh wheezed to the right with a scree of insects, and the path curved left over the river's lower bridge, its muddy banks thick and uneven like cookie dough. The breeze bounced against my shoulders and cheeks with the chill of night. Evening came on, and the purple winked with halogen eyes: girls should not be out alone anymore.

HOW TO DISAPPEAR AT PIZZA HUT

I did not excel as a Pizza Hut waitress. Our motto should have been "Bored Horny Teenagers Cook You Dinner." I tiptoed into the kitchen, steamy from the industrial dishwasher and crashing with the sounds of the round pans we used for deep-dish pizzas. The manager was always telling the cooks—boys got to be cooks, girls got to be waitresses—to quiet down, as their screams echoed out through the serving window and made the place feel less like a family establishment and more like a pirate ship.

I was glad I wasn't a cook. The cooks threw wads of dough at each other, were rumored to pee on the pizza, always seemed high, and had burns up and down their forearms from the oven, which was a large, long metal tunnel with a conveyor belt that carried the pizzas from one end to the other. When the belt got too full, pizzas would jam up at the lip of the oven and hold the ones at the back under the heat for longer, burning them. Sometimes the pans would align and buckle themselves in a long row, pushing the ones nearest the edge up and over the top and onto the floor.

New Lenox, Illinois, was once a small town that ran along the old Route 30, which hit I-80 just east of town. Pizza Hut, like almost every other business, was wedged in along Route 30, between a paint store and Maryland Fried Chicken. As a child, I gleefully went with my parents to pick up the greasy goodness of paper boxes filled with Maryland Fried Chicken. Across the gravel lot, Pizza Hut seemed to glower like a criminal outpost or maybe a strip club. Its windows were small triangular cutouts, and the roof looked like it was a hat pulled on too tight, so it seemed to me as a kid that something vaguely shady must have been happening inside.

By the time I was hired as a waitress there, Pizza Hut had moved to an open and more visible location at the corner of Vine and Route 30, one of the major unattractive crossroads in our town, with the Rust Belt to the east and the corn grid to the south and west. When I was younger, I'd lived up the hill on a cul-de-sac, and the second Pizza Hut location had been Sciniotes' car lot, where my dad once bought a used, navy-blue Chevy Monte Carlo we thought was terribly fancy. As a kid, I cut across the lot on my way to the newsstand in the town's only strip mall, where we bought Jolly Ranchers and five-cent blocks of Bazooka gum from plastic beach buckets arrayed along the counter.

———

As a teenager, I did not like making mistakes or making people unhappy, yet I stayed working at Pizza Hut for a year and a half during high school. The manager let me in early to open, and I stayed late to close, running through the degreasing procedure for the whole building as the manager turned the jukebox up. I didn't even really have friends there. My friends in high school were mostly on the math team.

My Pizza Hut coworkers included Coco, a girl a year older than me who was briefly hired as a waitress, though any of us could have told the managers that was a bad idea. Coco, who I believe was the unacknowledged 1980s inventor of vocal fry, was a cheerleader with wide blue eyes and a mass of blonde hair. She was like a cross between a human and a spider monkey, laughing in a kind of gravely squawk and flailing her arms and drinking pop and ordering elaborate pizzas and eventually getting accused of stealing money from the register.

I was in awe of the waitresses who stayed and who had been there before me, older girls who popped their gum and flirted with the customers, who had fancy rings of eyeliner—really so many layers to their makeup that their eyes looked like dark sparkling flowers, each blink of their eyelashes a kind of Venus flytrap. They would go on to get jobs at Chi-Chi's near the mall a few towns away, which had much better uniforms than we did. Ours were Holly Hobbie prim: a visor that everyone loathed, a poly-blend brown plaid short-sleeve shirt with ruffles near the neck, and polyester pants. The cooler waitresses spiced up the uniforms the best they could by opening all the buttons and leaning far over their tables.

There were lots of ways to hide at Pizza Hut. After I made the loop around my tables, took drink requests, and came back to key in the pizza orders on the boxy computers with the greasy keyboards, I'd nudge someone else out of the way to fill my drinks, pushing each plastic tumbler against the lever, waiting for the foam to go down, scooping the ice for the pitchers of pop. The drink station was large and substantial, tall, and it formed a wall between the waitstaff and the customers.

Later in life, at other jobs, I would learn that not being seen was a privilege. My job after Pizza Hut was at a video store, where I'd pour the popcorn kernels into the round hopper on the counter, and in a buttery fog, I'd answer the phone hanging on the wall. I'd work alone and rent porn tapes to the high school gym teacher with a smile while suppressing a gag. I'd answer the phone and listen as a man asked me to go into the back room and describe the covers of the adult movies. I'd hang up when I heard a wet regular sound. Some door from childhood slammed shut, but I didn't really feel violated. What was worse: I understood, or believed then, that I couldn't yell and tell him to fuck off. My bosses had paid for that hour of my life, and I set the phone firmly but silently on its cradle.

Within work's strictures, we are taught to stay still, not to move a muscle in the restraints of the time owned by someone else. In my early twenties at the photo store, a rich sixty-year-old grabbed my skirt because he "liked the fabric," then called to say we should date. I complained to the boss, who shrugged and said, "What do you want me to do?" I said drop him as a client and he refused, so I quit. And then I was without a job.

I signed up with a temp agency, Manpower, a name that now leers at me with a double meaning. The agency sent me to a roofing company, where I sat in a Plexiglas cubicle and alphabetized pink invoices while the sales guys threw videotapes of porn back and forth at each other across the space above their desks.

My next placement was at an HMO. I worked within health care while deeply resenting the fact that I wasn't insured.

I sat behind a laminate countertop in view of the patients and answered the phone, but I was told I couldn't read a book. When I was not actively responding to questions or calling to remind patients of their appointments, I was to sit and look into the empty middle space. This is the work of getting paid to be idle and yet standing at attention to serve. I gathered ideas or surreptitiously made notes for poems on small scraps of paper.

At Pizza Hut, there was no question about ever having the mental space to write down an idea. I just wanted to survive a shift without flinging a pizza into the salad bar, dropping an entire tray of drinks, or slipping on my ass in the greasy kitchen.

But one of the delightful things about Pizza Hut—I see only now—was that I was almost invisible. We had the shield of the pop machine, the shield of our weird visors and prim uniforms, and the shield of revenge. If customers were assholes, we would tell the cooks, and bad things were done to pizzas.

We had the shield of lying, too. Lying was such a necessary part of the job that I felt no guilt about adopting it as my own. "The oven broke," "Your pizza is coming right out," or, "My manager told me to give you a pizza for free." All these things could be arranged to make the customer happy or less irate, when the truth was that I'd stuffed my greasy, stained order pad into my apron pocket and forgotten to put in a pizza order twenty minutes ago, or a pizza had been destroyed in an unfortunate battle in the kitchen.

I make the cooks sound like nightmares, but they were also skilled practitioners of their art. They could fold a tall stack of pizza boxes with flying fingers, spread toppings evenly with a practiced gesture, and figure out ways to get a pizza out faster than seemed possible if you smiled at them sweetly or begged.

The pale gift of work is that it sometimes approaches play. Becoming one with a task—giving a lecture or crushing a cardboard box with an artful slit of the tape and swing of the foot—is a joy.

Rogue economist Thorstein Veblen sanded and smoothed the theoretical notion of "workmanship," claiming it as an instinct. The son of a Norwegian farmer, he fashioned this idea and lathed it in curls: humans, as they work on building a shelf or organizing a meeting, will naturally delight in handy, sensible, and beautiful improvements to the task at hand. He lauded the working instinct, running against the grain of philosophies devoted to tooth-and-nail and nasty-brutish-and-short.

I'd learned this gradually. In junior high, I collated and stapled papers for hours one summer day at the family business, watching the clock creep. Dad came in to pour a cup of bitter, overcooked Maxwell House, and I made a comment in boredom that I was not cut out for manual labor. He, with a lifetime of knowing in his eyes, said curtly but kindly, "There's nothing wrong with manual labor." A rare and pointed moment, as my dad was not one for guidance, it spun my world around, reorienting me like a compass. I knew this from the bottom up but not the top down. I knew it from the body, and now I knew it from the mouth and the mind.

What I meant with my statement to him, I think, was that I didn't want to staple things for my whole life and that I didn't know how to avoid that fate. I wanted to be a reporter for the

Joliet Herald, and I imagined that the way to get in the door was to be hired first as a custodian, and then somehow I would prove my worth.

I'd been working at assembly tasks in the office since seven or so, making leak test kits. Each began with a folded and printed cardstock folder. I would attach two plastic sleeves and slip a cotton swab in each. I'd staple the edge of each sleeve to the inside of a card-stock form and then staple a foil packet containing rubbing alcohol to the top. Somewhere on the receiving end, an important person, a man in a suit and lab coat, would catch the ball I threw. To test for radiation leaks on a piece of hospital or industrial equipment, my invisible partner would wipe first with the alcohol, then with the swabs, which would be sent back through a machine in the hallway, each swab in a little round container on a conveyor belt.

A nickel each, and also a nickel for making coffee in the morning. Soon, the folded kits would accumulate in a steady satisfying stack. The trick of fixing the misstapled, the sucking of the stapled finger, the figuring out of new tricks and positions to make things go faster—all of that would transfer to writing and to any other repetitive task I undertook. The satisfaction of a task broken down into parts, and once you do the parts, the whole approaches. Work-girl-ship.

I did, after a while, learn how to be a tolerable waitress. I learned that my shy smile meant good tips, a heavy apron of greasy crumpled bills and change resting against my thighs like armor. I loved to come home at night and count it.

I learned the routines for keying in pizzas, and I learned to take a big order in small pieces and soothe a grouchy table with free breadsticks and tomato sauce. I learned the pivot and swing of my tray. I learned how to stock the salad bar, and I still cut a green pepper in the way the Pizza Hut prep manual taught me. I still load the dishwasher in the same order that I bussed tables, silverware first.

My work—women's work, inside work—always meant I was lucky and should be grateful. I am grateful. Even if I was cleaning a toilet in Dad's office, I knew I was not standing below a cow as it was hoisted, bleeding, in the butchering shed—as Dad had. Even if I was cleaning up vomit in the Pizza Hut men's bathroom, I was not my German forebears, on the run from a miner's blacklist, forced to move to another cold-water shack to find a job in order to start trouble for another union. And then much later, my ex, a carpenter with thick-fingered and glorious hands, cut his eyes and mocked me: "You get to sit inside all day and press the letters of the alphabet while looking at a screen."

But this also mirrors the beginning of the head-fuck of work: *You should be grateful you have a job at all.* Work is bad, but the threat of no work is worse.

It's alarming in some ways to think that Pizza Hut has been one of my least stressful jobs. I dreaded going into most of my shifts, because I knew that for the hours I was there, I was not my own. I would have to survive it the best I could, and mistakes would be made. But once I was on shift, it was funny and sweaty and survivable, and the on-job expertise called "flow" kicked in, a kind of muscle memory and engagement, and then sometimes I got to be proud of myself for my quickness or for a big tip.

Within a year after Pizza Hut, I would learn that most bosses were not as nice as my fast-food managers. I learned that work, in its appropriated devilish form, means never being good enough and never being safe. At other restaurant jobs, this was almost expected: the boss who threw ice at the waitstaff, the groping from the cooks. At more than one white-collar job, I had very bad bosses. These men wore crisp shirts someone else had ironed; they called me into conference rooms to rage at me. I first got through it by blanking out, dissociating, and slinking off to cry. Later, I got through it by yelling back, calling on the various groups existing to support workers, documenting and filing grievances, and then driving home to cry in anger and humiliation.

———————

My managers at Pizza Hut were people who must have fallen down on their luck. Paul's eyes weren't quite right, and he seemed immersed in a fish tank behind his thick glasses. He forgot things; his shifts tended to spiral outward into chaos, and he would play the song "Electric Blue" by Icehouse on the jukebox over and over. Larry, a large, pale, balding man with glasses and a bemused smile, looked like he should have been an accountant, but he lived with his mom. Linda wore Band-Aids to hide the tattoos on the backs of her hands and ran each shift like a screaming roller coaster of efficiency. She should have been leading a country.

One night when I was out on the floor, carrying a pitcher of pop to a table near the windows, I stopped and turned with a swimmy slow-motion to see that somehow, at a booth near the salad bar, a gun had been drawn, a black shape. Larry strode out with the invisible customer-service conflict shield over his face.

The gun was put away, 911 was called, and Larry retrieved the pitcher of beer from the table. I could not fit the events in an order. I'd seen guns before, and one Arkansas relative traveled with a loaded gun beneath the seat of his truck, but I had not seen a person pull out a gun and point it at another person's face. The picture in my head of that moment is a blurred cutout.

Larry took care of everything, as if there were a page in the manual for this scenario: all the customers got their meals comped, half-finished pizzas were quickly slid into boxes and checks were voided, the police came, and then Larry closed the restaurant, letting us all go home without even emptying the trash.

The care with which this was all done—Larry had been the only adult in charge with a staff of teenagers—is something that I took at the time to be normal. Now I know there are a thousand stupid ways to deal with employees, including blaming whoever had served the table beer, or making us work the rest of the shift, or firing a scapegoat. Larry did none of these things. He asked us if we were OK, and we shrugged and said yes as we untied our aprons, pulled out our tucked-in shirts, and left.

―――――――

I wrote a whole novel in small spiral notebooks with light green pages while I was riding the subway to and from a stressful job in social work after college, and I started the novel purely because the job was making me so depressed that I cried every night. I needed another world to escape to; I needed another way to understand that I mattered. In that job, too, it was not the work itself but the shaming of management and the supervision that made it unbearable. To get release from the machinery of work-induced fear, I created a more compelling machine. Once I set this self-soothing in motion, the blank light-green pages became my refuge from the future and from failure, from all the bullshit of the next shift.

Assembly work and wage work have made me conscious that I can do anything for an hour. Like a little shift manager, when I write, I often make a note of my start time on a legal pad and then tell myself, *Just one hour.* Often, I'll get the engines revved up and go beyond that, but sometimes it's as automatic and artless as slapping cups and dirty plates into the pale blue racks of the Pizza Hut dishwasher. I bracket time to do my work in shifts, setting up the scaffolding and the schedule in which nothing much has to happen at all beyond the next right thing. My own work consumes and catches the minutes like an ever-growing stack of leak test kits.

I sometimes feel like I'm as good a writer as I was a Pizza Hut waitress; I'm not the most talented, but I sure do know how to show up for my next shift. And I love writing because I get to hide behind the wait station, avoiding the fear of other work and the accumulated salad bar of my own anxieties. I am not a very strict supervisor on my own shifts. I tell myself that all I need to do is drink my coffee and show up. Check social media, stare out the window if you want. Slap some shit on the page and you're fine. If it's a mess, we'll clean it up tomorrow.

In high school, I loved being invisible at Pizza Hut because in other arenas of my life, I was known, and things were expected of me. At home there was the continual fizz of family life with its conflicts, and at school there was the future, extending off blankly in some hazy direction that said only, "You must achieve more than stapling, somehow."

Despite this, I quit Pizza Hut abruptly after a year and a half. One slow afternoon, a regional manager came in for a kind of restaurant evaluation, and I was supposed to serve him—luck of the draw. He ordered an iced tea, and I brought it out, the top of straw's paper sleeve still covering its exposed end like a little hat. I brought two wedges of lemon in one of the little bowls we used for the breadstick tomato sauce. It was a slow afternoon and I had time for that bullshit.

The regional manager was impressed and gave me a good score, and Larry and Linda were so pleased. The next day, Linda, who did the schedules, put me all over the place, giving me the prize of more shifts—twenty hours a week. That's what everyone there wanted.

"No," I said the next day, a panic rising in my throat. I quit right there.

Linda's eyes scrunched up, pained and confused. She said she'd give me fewer shifts. She had been trying to reward me, not freak me out.

"No," I said. I didn't say what has taken me until now to figure out but what was an instinctive decision back then: I couldn't handle being too good of a waitress. I couldn't handle being known and therefore responsible for our shifts, for Pizza Hut store number whatever-we-were, for being relied on. I had come to rely on the routine of the place, on the chaos as a respite from a good-girl reputation that was choking every other arena of my young life and that would continue to be a problem.

If they gave me more shifts, I would take them, and then I would be swallowed in the attempt to do a job that I really didn't want to do. My precalculus grade would not survive that much Pizza Hut. But more than that, I sensed that it was dangerous for me to get too attached to my developing skills at Pizza Hut waitressing. So I left and took a slower job at the video store.

I learned how to quit when a job got too nasty. I learned that it was much less degrading to take my clothes off for money as an art model than when some old guy merely grabbed my skirt and chuckled. I learned that crying after work meant it was time to start circling new want ads. I'm a professor now, but what matters most for that job is my door—the privilege to choose when to be invisible.

I did not understand for years that Larry was in some ways the best boss I have ever had. He stayed out of our business and took care of us and laughed at us. When I quit, he said thank you and good luck with a smile and a sigh.

QUESTIONS ABOUT THE LAKEVIEW CAFÉ

How did Joe, an irritable former sergeant in the Turkish police, come to own a restaurant in a south suburban Chicago strip mall? Compared to the Turkish hillsides, did Chicagoland look horribly paved, ugly, and flat? And why did Joe hire me, the shyest waitress on the planet even after my Pizza Hut experience?

Joe ran the restaurant with Nicole, the Turkish head waitress whose Turkish name was Neval, and I was mystified by their relationship: Had they ever hooked up? Neval arrived for work, glamorous with bleached-blonde hair and pale-pink lipstick, but in the early mornings of her days off, she came in with no eye makeup, wearing sweatpants and clutching car keys, heading to pick up her daughter from her ex-husband. She never told me what she cried about those mornings.

Why did I feel trapped like a rat in a maze when I scurried along the narrow aisles with baskets of stale crackers and plastic-encased squares of butter? Joe made us wear white pants, but why did my cotton pair from Kmart make me feel like I was wrapped in a flour sack? Was it those pants that also led Neval to tell me I needed to lose weight around the ass?

I didn't know whether I was a woman then or a girl. Should I have called the smiling antennae repairman who ate lunch at the counter and left his number on a slip of paper under his coffee cup?

I polished the already-clean pink countertop in countless swirls of bleach-water. For some reason, it was more satisfying to refill the tables' square containers with paper packets of sugar and Sweet'N Low than to line the saltshakers on a tray, take off their silver tops, and pour salt into each open mouth. I wonder whether Joe appreciated that I cleaned the dusty domes of the hanging lamps with Windex and a rag. I had taken calculus in school, so why did I have such a problem with sales tax? I can't remember which mistake on a check made Joe yell and whip a handful of ice at my legs.

I don't know how the lesbian couple became regulars, with free meals and permanent seats at the back booth. I can't remember if I said much to either the older woman with glasses or the younger one with a shag haircut, though I knew they both worked at the antennae plant up the road, and they always greeted me as if they'd known me for years. How did Joe adopt them, or did they choose him? How did he choose the tiny grandmother with owlish glasses and the huge brown purse who also perched in the back booth and who they all called Mama? I wonder what happened to those friendships after the store was sold, after the pale pink and blue booths were ripped out to make way for a scrapbooking supply store or a tanning salon.

I wonder whether it broke Joe's heart to cook pale, soft open-faced turkey sandwiches on white bread with brown gravy for customers, and to serve broiled eggplant and Turkish delicacies only for the grandma, the lesbian couple, Neval, and me. When he cooked a huge plate of eggplant with chunks of spicy green pepper and potato for me, I wonder whether I adequately expressed my thanks.

I wonder whether it was legal for Joe to pay me two dollars an hour in cash. I imagine he did the same with Russ the cook and his nephew, shy Surrillo, the dishwasher. When

Russ grabbed my hand and refused to let go—we were in the kitchen amid red mesh bags of huge white onions—why did I freeze but only blush? When he mouthed the words "I love you" through the server window over orders of Denver omelets, how did I avoid his eyes? Russ and Surrillo must have known I was a college kid, that we had intersected in a universe that would never bring us together again.

Why did a huge table of Deadheads, following the band through concert tours and wearing expensive Guatemalan sweaters, find the Lakeview Café and order milkshakes during a lunch rush? For some reason, I'd wanted one of those sweaters when I first saw them on college peaceniks, but then I gasped when I fingered the price tag on one during a trip to Minneapolis. And more importantly, what was it about peace, love, and being high that caused them to drop my tip, all in coins, into the pale brown soup of their melted backwash ice cream in the tall shake glasses? Did they think this would freak me out? Ruin my day? And why do I remember it still? I suppose this keen flash of memory comes as the pointed fishhook to the bait that the hippies might promise a new life.

I wonder what it was about Neval's recipe for rice pudding that was so incredible. I wonder why she served me dish after dish of cream-rich pudding with cinnamon-dusted skin while encouraging me to lose weight. I wonder who suggested the name Lakeview Café, when there was no lake anywhere, only a massive parking lot that was lake-like in its grayness and with the seagulls that wheeled above, looking for French fries and trash.

LAND OF
INFINITE DAVID

"Look at that," said Mr. Carroll, my high school history teacher. He either pointed or just squinted at the gray strip of highway that led south into the ocean-bottom flatness of rural Illinois. "That's your future."

Clouds bunched against the press of sky like the underside of a luminous table stuck with wads of gray gum. Highway exits curved outward into the corn grid of industrial vegetables grown for their chemical components. The highway narrowed to a hazy point at the horizon as blank as the silence I offered, a confusion so deep that it would not cohere into a reply.

He meant to inspire, I think, to make me remember. And even now I see this vision in grays. But the moment was like a career aptitude quiz designed to awaken new hope that instead aggravated old dread and stirred further hopelessness, like the test printout with its inscrutable oracles: *Consider careers in agricultural communications or children's entertainment.* Our journey in Mr. Carroll's Suburban would lead to a chipped-concrete, central Illinois college campus, one facet of a day and a year and a young life in which adults made comments like this without explaining them.

The tires whined over a swath of ridged rumble-strip highway, and the van jolted every minute or two against splotches of asphalt patch jobs and sections of uneven pavement. Cold pinched the dust where glass met plastic in the far reaches of the Chevy Suburban in 1988. Someone had spray-painted the words "Trust Jesus" on every bridge embankment that cut across the highway. The script was always the same, with the letters stacked in two layers, five columns. You could look for hours at that phrase on each overpass until the words dissolved into letters, and the imagined early morning scene of a faceless speaker leaving this graffiti felt like the loneliest thing in the entire world.

———————

When writer David Foster Wallace killed himself in late 2008, the Illinois in me got rung like a bell. I was apparently the only person who didn't even know he'd grown up in Philo on I-57, the town next to Champaign-Urbana, where his father taught at the University of Illinois. I had read *Infinite Jest* much too quickly and impatiently in a post-undergraduate haze but somehow picked up the impression that Wallace was East-Coasty, brilliantly born in Ithaca, probably bred in Manhattan with summers in Connecticut and prep school in New Hampshire. Then he died. With his obituary like rain on the slick windshield of my screen, I swerved through work but couldn't let that weather lift. Why he committed suicide was, on one level, easy to answer. But beyond that was the guilt. I worried about my small role in his large murder.

He taught at Illinois State University after *Infinite Jest* came out. I worried that the bleak flatness of an Illinois winter had killed him, that between the East Coast and his sojourn in California at Pomona College, he stayed too long and the sadness seeped in. I worried that somehow, by the transitive property, I was partially to blame. I am not a glacier, of course, nor a crafter of large swathes of geography. But as an obviously

Olympic-contender codependent and a lifelong maker of helpful flyers and bullet-pointed signs, I worried that we in the state of Illinois knew about the crashing, soul-crushing nature of our state and—as usual—said too little. I worried that he had not been adequately warned.

I worried I should have written a letter to my former state senators. Dear Formerly Alive, Formerly Bow-Tied Senator Paul Simon: Maybe tollbooth operators should hand out pamphlets to brilliant depressives, such as "Wondering about How Illinois Will Affect Your Mental Health?"

This pamphlet might warn against common myths. Even if you think you know what you're getting into, this version of the Midwest is not the Scandinavian heaven of good music and culture in Minnesota. It is not a Dakota purity of flatness and cold, not Iowa the island, not Michigan the outdoorsy mitten, not silly Indiana stuck in its own racetrack, and not Ohio with its self-contained universe of semi-big "C" cities. There is something more complex in the Illinois geographic bottleneck of travel—its north-southness, its Chicago-and-not-Chicago self-hatred, its road trip necessity, its Manhattan-Project-Reagan-and-Rumsfeld-birthplace shame, its license-plate-Land-of-Lincoln-but-not-Lincoln's-birthplace *almostness*—that might leave a person of a certain need abandoned out in the cold somewhere in the corn grid. And apparently, this is all explained in Wallace's *Westward the Course of Empire Takes Its Way*, a novella I had not yet read when he died. Still, as an Illinois-almost, I venture to say something small as Philo, as simple as New Lenox.

That day in Mr. Carroll's Suburban, we were on our way to some honors history conference at Illinois State University in Bloomington-Normal or at Western Illinois University in Macomb or at the University of Illinois in Champaign-Urbana. These events, where we would listen to panels about the Black Death or present our skits about the *Epic of Gilgamesh* or Plato's Elysian Fields, seemed to have been designed to titrate out the five nerdiest students from our junior class of over seven hundred students. And I clung to them—and to the math team weekend competitions, timed worksheets, and trophies for Venn Diagrams—because "cool" in our school meant heavy metal, and tons of eyeliner softened with the flame of a plastic lighter, and then disappearing into the grid, where destiny meant getting up at 6:00 a.m. to turn on the defroster and chip ice off your windshield.

High school history teachers were the smartest people I knew. Earlier that year, I had visited Mr. Miller, my sophomore history teacher and my hero, who was sweet and kind, curly-headed and hilarious. I sat in his cramped office—which he shared with five other teachers, stuffed to the ceiling with papers and projects, unwindowed and grim—and I unfolded my future shyly, the treasure of my admiration. "I want to be just like you," I told him, "a high school history teacher." I wanted to go to the University of Illinois or Illinois State, attend a college with "Normal" in the name, which I knew meant a teacher's college. I would take on that noble work. I felt the security and relief of finding access to normal, of choosing a calling.

Mr. Miller lowered his brows over his blue eyes and shook his head. "No," he said. "No. You can do better." Ice-blue eyes searing me, so stern and almost angry, with something desperate in the way he slammed shut that door for me, knowing my reverence for him and that my obedience would never allow me to open it again. It was my first Zen koan of Illinois flatness. I wanted to weep. I probably did later. He left me to wander rather than telling me to obey.

My future was the problem, and "future" means "your job." The solution was the road. I knew this from my father's story; work was the reason Dad moved from Subiaco, Arkansas, north to St. Louis and then to New Lenox. When Mr. Carroll offered his solution by pointing south through the windshield, he seemed to condemn me to reverse my family's northward ambitions. "Wait," I wanted to say, "the city is the other way." Our list of books to read for college seemed to be all about road trips to find work. I read Upton Sinclair's *The Jungle*, about immigrants moving to work in the Chicago stockyards, and Edna Ferber's *So Big*, about a destitute farm girl who heads to Chicago in poverty and hope, gets destroyed there, and heads back home. We were always aware of Chicago's compass point as a North Star, as a place where fires were made and put out. In high school, we routinely drove to the city at night (sorry, Ma) with no destination in mind at all. We had no idea what kind of place we would want to visit in the city and no idea where to find—inside us or in print or on faces—the kinds of things we might really like to do.

But mostly we drove to other places out on the corn grid, just like Wallace, who traveled the state as a tennis player. His essay "Derivative Sport in Tornado Alley" catalogs how success and mobility unfold through the windshield from towns like

Champaign and Danville, like Pekin, "insurance hub and home of Caterpillar Tractor; like the Midwest Junior Clay Courts at a chichi private club in Peoria's pale version of Scarsdale." We took long bus rides to do the things that mathletes and history club kids and band nerds do. We arrived and took our tests and played our songs and read our presentations from nervous, sweat-stained notecards, and we always got our asses kicked by high schools in the northern suburbs like New Trier, where both Donald Rumsfeld and Charlton Heston went to school.

And when we were not performing or aiming for the blank ahead, we drove aimlessly because the future was always somewhere else, because Illinois is a road trip and cannot be otherwise. Furling interstates wind around Chicago like a necklace, then curl southward at various angles toward St. Louis, where they are cinched at the state's hip. Illinois is Miss America in a pretty dress, a ball gown colored the lime-electric green of the fields in spring, with accents of pale purple chicory and a sash in the gray fabric of highway gravel.

Every highway angle from Chicago to someplace else is a comforting chunk of your life measured in hours, like the five-hour diagonal toward St. Louis. As a child, I rode through Philo several times a year on I-57. I never waved. We made the eleven-hour trip down to western Arkansas, crossing the southern border of Illinois at Charleston, south of St. Louis. The highways faded to late nights in the back seat, the smell of vinyl and the neon of travel plaza signs and the blur of sleep. We curled tight like puppies to protect ourselves from the cold and dreamed of the slightly sweet smell of exhaust, the crinkle of fast-food wrappers. When we woke in the early pink, we watched for the green signs at the roadway's right, straining to see the name of the next city and the number of miles, learning to divide by sixty to figure out the time, believing that keeping track would make the time either shrink or become more our own. In many senses, Mr. Carroll was right. That highway formed the eyes and the head that would make and see my future. It was my future because it was my past, my spine.

———————

After David Foster Wallace died, my boyfriend Cliff brought me a book from the library that I had not known existed before: *Everything and More: A Compact History of Infinity*. The book lofted way over my head into college math and beyond but left me thrilled and adoring. It was this lovely little book, part math history, part math humor, and partly the mechanics of Zen spirituality as the alphabet soup of infinity, that sealed my devotion. This was long before I learned that Wallace had thrown a coffee table at Mary Karr, long before he was consigned with so many others to the asymptotic territory of never-safe.

Wallace's clear obsession with the abstract and visual elegance of functions and calculus, and the struggle to explain the weirdness of the internal and external universes, showed him to be brilliant in a grinding, all-the-way-to-the-bottom fashion. I felt a gentle kinship with a man who loved the asymptote, one of those references you could try to work into conversation endlessly as a joke that always fell flat. Asymptotes are curved lines that approach an axis but never actually cross it, doing a sort of dance with their guiding line, the same way a road like I-57 seems to cross the Illinois horizon but never does.

———————

In his "Derivative Sport" essay, Wallace traces the geography of Illinois, "the sharp intercourse of straight lines," his love of tennis, and the weather in Tornado Alley, a segment of eastern Illinois buffeted with lake-effect extreme weather and wind: "The Illinois combination of pocked courts, sickening damp, and wind required and rewarded an almost Zen-like acceptance of things as they actually were, on-court. I won a lot."

In that part of Tornado Alley, where I also grew up, the twisters appear and zigzag like irrational functions on a sheet of graph paper. A tornado once tore through Joliet the day before I had an orthodontist appointment there. I followed detours that led past mountains of smoking rubble. I passed a smoldering ditch, an improbably intact tanning salon, blocked roads, and flashing red lights. Bulldozers moved back and forth meditatively. As they pushed spindly piles of ripped boards and snaking metal, their shovels rose and fell toward the center as if they were bowing. One house sat turned on its foundation. Another house with white aluminum siding was peeled like a banana.

The stereotype of the Midwest is zero, nothing. The stereotype of Zen is peace, calm, a sales-pitch sip of green tea in a cruise-ship spa. Anyone who does meditation knows that it is an industrial, hard-edged, bottomless encounter with their roaring mind, and also that it can become jade-plant succulent. Novelist George Saunders described Wallace as "a great American Buddhist writer," and Wallace's unfinished novel, *The Pale King*, gives us IRS employees sorting through tax forms toward an awareness born of sustained concentration at the particulars of this sometimes too-regular, sometimes too-gridded, sometimes too-flat life. Wallace imagines them breaking through the grid into the ecstasy beyond.

Wallace left a typed note about the unfinished novel: "Bliss—a-second-by-second joy and gratitude at the gift of being alive, conscious—lies on the other side of crushing, crushing boredom. Pay close attention to the most tedious thing you can find (Tax Returns, Televised Golf) and, in waves, a boredom like you've never known will wash over you and just about kill you. Ride these out, and it's like stepping from black and white into color. Like water after days in the desert. Instant bliss in every atom."[1]

In the late 1980s, as I drove the grid in high school loops, Wallace left Philo, Illinois, to drive east to Amherst College in Massachusetts. The *New Yorker* provided a kernel about his departure: "Before Wallace left for college, he took a long walk through the cornfields, to say goodbye to the Midwest."[2]

You say secret things to corn. You cannot have an easy relationship with it if you know Illinois. You know it is the reason for the nitrate-saturated groundwater and the runoff and soil erosion and the creeks that foam with green bubbles and the economic viability of the small towns that trapped and nonetheless bred you. Yet you are intoxicated with that beefy earth-and-biology smell in the springtime, sex coming right from the ground, as if the corn itself is flipping the bird in even rows to the factory farms and saying, "Despite our utter domestication, we can still give off the elixir of wild, raw, monocot joy." You hide in the corn and trip on the cornrows and scan the horizon for threshers that will eat you up. You know Malachai and the other Children of the Corn live somewhere in the rows. You hear the warnings of "don't get

1 Jennifer Schuessler, "Our Boredom, Ourselves," *New York Times*, Jan. 21, 2010.
2 D. T. Max, "The Unfinished," *New Yorker*, March 9, 2009.

lost in there, you'll lose your bearings when you can't see above the tassels," and you believe them.[3] You can never remember: is it "knee-high by the Fourth of July" or "high as an elephant's eye by the Fourth of July?" And you can't ask anyone because that is like forgetting your second cousin's name. You ride past the blurring rows, watching from the school bus window, and the green becomes the blur of days, and the rows spread out and collapse like a hypnotizing, magic fan as you pass.

If I had known about Wallace in 1989, I could have pegged myself as a slavish copycat. After the ride in Mr. Carroll's Suburban came the college applications. I attended a college like Amherst, but in the Midwest, because the brochures had nice fall foliage and heavy cardstock and pictures of kids playing frisbee, and so I thought, OK. Then, after college, I decided to move to the East Coast because—because why? I don't know. Because life happens out there on the edges.

Wallace moved to Boston in 1989, where he had a breakdown and ended up on a locked psychiatric ward at McLean's Hospital. He lived in nearby Somerville and in a halfway house in Brighton. He became immersed in Boston's recovery community. He moved to Syracuse, finished *Infinite Jest*, and got a job at Illinois State University in 1993. He said he was happy to return to the Midwest. *Infinite Jest* came out in 1996.

Wallace was brilliant and troubled, and I was working retail and popping Klonopin and thinking I could handle being a

3 The first version of the film (1984) was shot in the area of Sioux City, Iowa. The second, made-for-television version, directed by Donald P. Borchers, was filmed in the Quad Cities area of Illinois, which lies two hours due west of New Lenox on Interstate 80. "Children of the Corn," *The Internet Movie Database*.

social worker. I moved to Boston in 1993 and lived in Allston, next to Brighton, and in Somerville. I worked as a counselor, visited my patients at McLean's Hospital. I became immersed in Boston's recovery community, first by ferrying my charges to Narcotics Anonymous meetings, then by ferrying myself to a group for the families and friends of alcoholics and addicts to deal with my own recurring history and penchant for close association with those folks. I just missed Wallace, though I'm sure his brilliance would have made me too shy to ever even say hello. In 1998, I moved back to Illinois.

My time in Boston thumped with the bassline of a forlorn song: "Oh, Illinois." Away from the Midwest, I stumbled almost immediately upon the thing people kept drawing my attention to: the midwestern accent (*Are you from Chicago?*) and the flannel (*Wow, how did you end up here?*). Without meaning to, I became the worst midwestern missionary, first defending it like a surly child, flashing a slight scowl and an awkward silence at a potluck when someone made a dismissive comment. Then I could laugh about it and describe it as a place to go to instead of just a place to endure on Interstate 80. But I played the hick schtick when I could have just left it alone. I told people as only a half-joke that *Wayne's World* was my favorite movie, laughed and said, "Oh, the Midwest isn't that bad" when what I wanted to tell them about was the ecstasy of starlings against lilac sky, waving corn tassels, warehouses and truck stops that held a particular kind of silence.

And so because of my shame, it has taken me an essay to work shyly toward what others probably know, but I need to present it as if it's something fancy, like the Fabergé egg encrusted with the roadway glitter of smashed-windshield jewels: Illinois is the land of David Foster Wallace in his brilliance and his brokenness and his violence. He was born in Ithaca, New York, but Illinois is the land he claimed as his own, and I understand one piece of myself through the lens of him, he who takes the idea of cows-on-the-book-cover and farm-town bucolic and stares at these ideas until they dissolve into exhaust. Birth does not equal destiny, but landscape helps produce the soul over time. Rest in peace, son of the corn, cousin to tornadoes.

HOMAGE
TO A BRIDGE

A metal worker cast each letter of a seventeen-line poem into bronze and maybe started with a shopping list: thirty-seven As, thirty-eight if you count the author's name.

Another worker, skilled at wedding alloys, calculated the weld strength, solder, and flux needed to melt the bronze to the steel of a bridge. A construction crew puzzled over the blueprints, fitted girders into a network of triangles and squares above rushing lanes of Minneapolis highway traffic, laid the fir planks, then sprayed the structure dusty blue and pale vanilla.

"Hey, honey, you'll never guess what I did today at work. I built a poem."

———————

The poem starts at the bridge's west edge. Understated three-inch letters, broad and stately, dot the girders like the marks on a ruler. The letters hang against a backdrop of sky ten feet above the walkway. The weight and speed of cars on the sixteen-lane highway below sets the bridge into constant, subtle vibration enveloped in a gentle buzz of rubber on asphalt. You must move to see the poem, and the world moves beneath you as the sky shifts above.

When the poem is half over, the stairway appears, leading down to Loring Park. Either double back to follow the rest of the poem, which stretches above the walkway's opposite edge, or go about your business, with the first half dangling between your ears, waiting for resolution.

If you don't know what you're doing, you might dash across the bridge and jump into the poem's middle. The shock of poetry on a bridge might blur your vision so you scarcely read the words. You don't even let yourself savor the whole poem or take it in. The world's panic and light-splinters might pepper your eyes if you are a nineteen-year-old midwestern shell-shocked girl, if you take the bridge like a runway or a trespass, gulping air and letters, stopping beside a sentence that lodges itself in your head.

The cold wind pushes strands of long brown hair into your mouth, tangling and wrapping around your glasses. The need for a Kleenex and a bathroom, maybe over there in the Loring Park Café. Hate to hurry through a restaurant to pee like a thief when you know you won't buy coffee. Late to meet someone. Burr of tires on pavement. One of the memories collected by all of your skin and organs, not just your eyes.

A poem on a bridge. The only thing I remember about it was either a line or a threat:

AND IT IS GOOD WHEN YOU GET TO NO FURTHER

The Irene Hixon Whitney Bridge, also called the Friendship Bridge, spans Lyndale Avenue, Hennepin Avenue, and Interstate 94. Siah Armajani, the artist who designed it, was born in Iran and has been creating large usable works since the 1970s. Fascinated and transfixed with bridges as public sculpture, he designed the bridge's prototype in 1985, and the structure was completed in 1988.

Armajani wanted to make the bridge's pale yellow the same color as that which Thomas Jefferson used at Monticello. The yellow half of the bridge is to the east, and the western half is blue. The two colors overlap in a pair of harmonic waves that incorporate the three most common forms of the American bridge: the suspension bridge, which looks like a Golden Gate-Brooklyn peak with lines hanging down; the long horizontal trestle, boxes with Xs in the middle that make you think of railroad bridges; and the inverted arch, the swoop of a downward moon, a gentle hill. It might sound messy, but the bridge has a calm personality. The standard intervals and proportions support the hybrid form, like a person with wild ideas who still knows how to tie her shoes and schedule dental visits.

Armajani asked poet John Ashbery to create a poem for the 379-foot span linking the Walker Arts Center and Sculpture Garden to downtown Minneapolis.

The bridge was two or three years old when I stepped onto it for the first time. The poem wasn't meant for me; don't touch the librarian girl, shoulders curled inward like a closed fist. What were mine were giveaways and thrift-store finds, things left on the curb for the trash.

A freshman at rural Carleton College south of Minneapolis, I drove up to the city with women from my dorm to see the Walker Arts Museum because it was the thing to do and we were doing it, impressing each other with our hardiness and then mirroring the savvy we wanted to have in each other's eyes. We wandered through the Minneapolis Sculpture Garden, which covers the top of the city in a landscaped quilt, arranged in imaginary squares like a garden from *Alice in Wonderland*, with trellises and arches of green, a bronze bunny leaping, a gazebo of space junk, and a famous sculpture of a massive shiny cherry on a pop art spoon, slicked with trickling water.

I snapped a picture of the poem's haunting line a few years later. I held up my plastic point-and-shoot camera and fit the sentence, "AND IT IS GOOD WHEN YOU GET TO NO FURTHER," in my lens, with the backdrop of a wispy cold midwestern sky marked with mare's-tail clouds, the afternoon light radiating a hint of gold.

Inscriptions on architecture usually trace the top outer edge of large, publicly funded buildings like a library or a statehouse, and they seem to speak to the sky, not to little humans. Those words, often in Latin, are created through absence; their meaning comes from stone that's not there anymore, like the hollowed-out pupil in an ancient Roman statue's eye.

This bridge is the inverse: you are contained within a poem inside a space that isn't a shelter at all. The letters extend toward you into the air, spanning a bit of the distance, holding themselves off their metal page.

After I took the picture of the bridge, I got the film developed at a drugstore somewhere in Minnesota. Around that time, events took their natural unraveling course. I left school after a summer of depression and panic attacks, joined an anarchist collective, shaved my head. I got by, eating free bread from the bakery at closing time. Don't worry about that girl, though: it's OK. I was a very orderly anarchist, always a functioner, a list-maker. There is coffee, there is free art in gardens, there is the midwestern sky. The tragedy story is not mine. Mine is the library, the gentle golden story of seeking and finding quiet.

The picture I took of my sentence got tucked in a cardboard box of important scraps: art projects, literary journals with a few of my poems, pieces of ribbon and buttons with political slogans, my ratty first concert T-shirt, old letters and prizes from gumball machines. In the years that followed, I sorted through that treasure box each time I moved to a new city or across an old city to a new apartment. In the pre-move paring-down and winnowing, I would squat in an empty room and examine the picture, always struck differently by the sentence, the colors of the sky behind it, the lost moment that caused me to capture a piece of a poem, the way it spoke each time to the particular *no further* where I found myself.

You know nineteen and twenty: busting out of your skin, when the libraries and museums needed people screaming and dashing down the halls. The only presence that held me was the close press of other bodies in a mosh pit or at a demonstration, sweating and thrashing or yelling and jumping. After both, you're hoarse, your ears ring. Your body's changed, good-exhausted. The quiet of the day and early evening was much harder, but people built bridges. Wasn't it funny and wild?

———————

Ekphrastic poetry is poetry about a piece of art. John Ashbery writes a lot of that kind of poetry, so it was fitting that Armajani asked him to write a poem for a bridge.

One of Ashbery's most famous books of poetry, *Self-Portrait in a Convex Mirror*, is written in response to a painting of the same name by Francesco Mazzola, known as Parmigianino. The painting turned Renaissance Italy upside down; it was painted not on canvas but on a wooden sphere to accurately portray the shape distortions of the image as reflected by a glass ball. One line of the title poem challenges "those assholes / Who would confuse everything with their mirror games." Ashbery's poem rocked the literary world of 1976, and prizes were showered down upon him.

As a young poet in the 1950s, Ashbery had lived in Paris, writing for *ARTnews* to earn extra money. He didn't like being tagged as an art critic, though, and he said, "I've always tried to avoid telling people what to do. So it's rather ironical that I've ended up being both a critic and a teacher, and am forced to assume this role. But I don't feel that I in most cases really know what people should do, whether they're artists or students, and it's a bit of a strain having to pretend that I do know."

I read articles about the bridge that quoted Ashbery's poem, but no one quoted my line. Many people like the line, "This far, it is fair to be crossing, to have crossed."

———————

And it is good when you get to *no further*.

I returned to the bridge in 1991 at twenty, like the scene of a crime I couldn't remember committing but felt guilty about anyway.

The line in that poem, the only one that stuck in my head, was the hollow deep tone of a single church bell, a call to a funeral. No further: a bottomless moment defining all of the others, like the death of a child. Like the death of one Iraqi child in the desert that year, like the demonstrations that snaked their way around the buildings of downtown Minneapolis in the cold, the shouts echoing off the glass of skyscrapers, "No Further." Those shouts said, *No further: we will take no more*, but seemed to also mean, *We have no tricks, no new tools left in our bags.*

It's silly to wonder about the future when the desert's on fire. I went through pills, panic, and the hospital. I left school that year, but not to write a book about my wandering, which was only a construction story of burst pipes and joists that had to be replaced before the room could be rebuilt. The point was to hide the traces and seams, to get the stains and water damage gone.

The important thing, I thought, was that nobody hit a real bottom at twenty. You couldn't be lonely enough at twenty for it to really count.

A year later, *no further* meant driving in the car with all my possessions in the back seat, having just thrown up all over the steering wheel after trying to live on discounted kale and half-rotten bagels from the clearance section of the food co-op. I stripped down and threw my jeans and shirt into a dumpster behind a grocery store, wiped myself off with fast-food napkins from the glove compartment, found another pair of jeans and a shirt in my duffle bag. I cleaned off in the sink of a coffee shop bathroom.

That was not my rock star moment. It seemed then that there was plenty more and deeper *no further* to find, all waiting ahead of me. The horrible thing about *no further* is exactly the fact that no one tells you when you've reached it. Imagine the comfort of knowing it won't ever get any worse than it already is.

The worst part was the phrase "And it is good": the ultimate Zen fuck-you, as if the punishment was deserved on a universal level, even if you only half-understood what you'd done.

One stairway of the bridge touches down on Loring Park, which at one time was edged to the north by the long and lean Loring Park Café, a hip sprawling coffee shop, that, in the early nineties, was decked out in a tented, lush-pillowed fantasy. I knew one of the waitresses there, Greta, an earthy actor with a husky cigarette voice who was in my anarchist study group.

I got lucky, jumping out of school into a net of anarcho-punks who broke my fall. I worked at a coffee shop and we read Murray Bookchin's *Post-Scarcity Anarchism* and I did not understand much. But Cindy and Laura and Greta and Liza had short, buzzed hair that made you want to rub your palm across their scalps. They made their own clothes and stir-fry dinners and collectives.

I learned that if you were feeling silly or bold, you could take your shirt off at a demonstration and yell. There was a radical bookstore in a storefront basement near the University of Minnesota. We held an anarchist party, baked a cake for the Haymarket Martyrs killed by the Chicago police, "In November We Remember." We made stickers for every occasion, composed strange little street theaters for bus stops, took over a corner of Kinko's at 2:00 a.m.: this circle is liberated space.

It's fucking great when you're pushed against the wall and you light a bomb like Emma Goldman.

Breathless: And it is *good* when you get to no further. And you can say *no further* like, *hell no, we won't go.* Like, *I'd prefer not to.* Like, *I like my coffee with cream and my public transportation fully funded and democratically controlled.* Like, *let's fight for it.* We were at the same time all falling apart, wanting to leave the city or maybe finish our degrees or get jobs, needing to go to the doctor or get our teeth fixed, saving our pennies for therapy or to buy a car to get the fuck out of this miserable city. I couldn't be that rebel, couldn't be Emma, because I was too shy and screwed up in the head. But I could read about her, absorb her.

We made anarchist zines and flipped through books of clip art to make our posters. If you found a book on anarchism in the clearance bin of the used bookstore, it might have a tattered plain jewel-blue cover and be called *Anarchism in Fin-de-Siècle Paris*, and it would be about the coffee shops and salons where the bombmakers traded seditious ideas, about how Dada and Surrealism took the moment, the magical moment, and tried to seize it for another consciousness, for a moment of *wake up*, a moment of social *no further.* The surrealists arose in response to World War I's wanton destruction behind André Breton's hope for a new vision that might be guided less by plans and more by dreams.

Out of this came a 1960s art movement called Fluxus. The Walker Art Center, with the Armajani bridge in its front yard, hosted a large retrospective exhibit of Fluxus in 1992 or 1993.

Rick Salafia, an art instructor and conceptual sculptor, drove us around the state for his sculpture classes, to junkyards, second-hand stores, and lumberyards, so privileged college kids could smell the sawdust and see the material from its source. He put planers and chisels in the hands of rich kids from New York City and made them build tables. He showed us slides about Fluxus and Dada. He rented a van and drove us up to the Walker for the Fluxus exhibit, where we saw photos and recreations of the performance art work of Joseph Beuys and Yoko Ono's apple on top of a stepladder.

In that white, lit space, I stopped in front of a glass case that contained a many-compartmented box made by Joseph Cornell, a self-taught artist. The box seemed to contain pieces of a game with no rules: compartments for a yellow ball and a parakeet, tiny containers and clouded vials. Together, these pieces had a harmony that didn't whack you over the head with meaning. The box's size and portability, its ability to conceal its contents and to pass as any other cardboard box, promised both humility and intelligence, made promises too about life in general and the way that treasures are concealed. The compartments were regular enough to mirror the geometric interlocking of molecules that compose us and the whole wide world. It said, *look, we've got chaos, but we also have foundations.*

Back in school, I got a job as a model for a drawing class and came in to see the students' sketches of me in a line along the studio wall, and I knew for the first time that I was a real person; after all, there was the evidence. I made much bad art, and Rick gave me bad grades. He let me learn how to weld, and like a character in a novel, I made a huge, metal book from the tailgate of a red Ford pickup I found in a junkyard, as if to resolve my thematic conflicts. He let me do an independent study in sculpture where I made strange wall hangings and dolls out of men's neckties I bought at the thrift store.

Rick met with me in his quiet office and paid attention. He pointed at what I made, said, "Here, look at the knotted hand on this doll. It's perfect." And then a dry question, a pushing further, a book to read, an image. I tried to have a crush on him because he gave me a new way to see the world, but my heart slipped off, hung up only where it was surgically appropriate. He knew about dealing with troubled college girls. And yet we had his full attention. He never mocked us and our ridiculousness.

Walking in a throng of people with my black polyester and cardboard graduation cap in my hand, Rick stood, waiting in an area roped off with ribbon. He watched our class approach beneath the canopy of waving green oak. He gave me a hug, a brief serious gaze from his still eyes. He let his pudgy worn face smile, and he said, "You were the only student who got an A+ from me."

Rick, I carried that yellow ball, that golden kernel of respect, in a Fluxus box near my chest, pocket-sized, for ever more. Later, when I was so down my forehead was on the wood floor, clutching the receiver and on hold with some rape crisis hotline or emergency mental health counselor, the A+ was one of two or three pearls I touched on a private rosary.

Rick was a separate bead on a precious string of men who taught me about making things and finding the self. Did these men (more than two, less than ten) feel the pressure in their interactions with me of having to remake my relationship with the world? Was it heavy lifting for them to bear my presence as they steadfastly behaved appropriately and with respect? Where is it written on their records that they were good, as in "good men," as in the kind of men that reveal the existence of trustworthiness without using that halo to blind you while the other hand strokes your leg?

"Good" could mean the yowl at a demo, but it could also mean your own quiet space, an empty room where you can get to no further. You stop and consider, with the light streaming in, nearer to making a decision and on the verge of starting something new. Like a Fluxus box with empty compartments, you get to choose what goes inside, and no one can tell you what it means. And that is good.

———————

As a ten-year-old boy, John Ashbery discovered surrealism—revealing the treasures of the subconscious to try to save the world—and Cornell's boxes.

He read a *Life* magazine article about a show on surrealism at the Museum of Modern Art in New York. "I'm not sure whether Cornell's boxes were included in the show, but after reading *Life* and discovering that I was a surrealist, I found pictures of his work in books on surrealism at the local library," he writes in a book about the artist.

Ashbery was twenty-two when he first saw Cornell's boxes in an exhibition: "There it was all intact, the reserves of childhood seeing protected, arranged behind glass and protected also by the unfathomable intent of the mysterious artist behind it."

After corresponding with Cornell for *ARTnews*, Ashbery traveled to the artist's home in Flushing, New York, to meet him. Cornell lived in a tiny, drab house, Ashbery writes, in "several rooms that seemed crammed with tiny objects, both unusual and extraordinary; strange antique toys as well as more recent pedestrian ones that might have been giveaways from a local filling station." Ashbery writes that they listened to a record of French piano music, drank Lipton tea, and ate heavy pastries.

———————

And it is good when you get to no further.

I unpacked my box of accumulated treasures and found the photo once more, in a new apartment with a new fiancé in a new state. If you are a stubborn student, the *when* implies a repetition of the sort that would have been horrifying to think about at twenty—before the alcoholic, before the first and second and third almost-marriages and the cruelty that was unleashed when these dissolved like spun sugar in water.

The curves of the colored paths on the game board become familiar, like acing Candyland or Chutes and Ladders. You pass "Go" and there you are. *No further* becomes a kind of home, and you round the bend with centrifugal force bringing you ever closer. Getting to *no further* becomes almost routine, despite your resolutions to progress.

Then you have a baby and you slip down the rabbit hole into the bowels of the earth, where *no further* is the gritty threat of your child's vanishing and your own soul vanishing with him.

Here is *no further*, with an emphasis on the "no" that will tattoo you for the rest of your life: fighting with baby's dad, screaming in madness and anger, and the one-year-old baby is clutched between you, laughing his pink laugh with anxiety in his eyes because he cannot comprehend his parents' twisted faces. You are running through the house, tossing bibs and diapers and socks into a duffle bag, snacks for a long spontaneous road trip of rage, and you clutch a breakable item you want to throw. In the kitchen, you are caught in a tornado of yelling, and you wake, realize the baby is gone in the August heat.

The front door is open. You dash out, feet not touching the ground, and you see him toddling off down the sidewalk. You live in a rough neighborhood, and the baby is stumbling off to say hello to the house of addicted young men next door. Not that you begrudge them their private hell, but now . . . now you are going to yours. That moment: you clutch that child, into the car seat he goes, a part of you is spinning a web faster and faster around the alternate path where the baby is gone. Numbly, you drive.

This is *good* in the wicked sense of a roaring universe screaming at you about your own extinction. To be aware of that is good. You get a large Buddhist wrathful protector deity tattooed on your shoulder, a fanged orange woman with a ritual knife, and for the hours of the three sessions in the tattoo studio, you welcome the scarring and the lines of precise pain, nothing like the volcano of childbirth, and you hope it will teach you a lesson, will draw a magic line between you and all of those *no furthers*. This isn't an epiphany; this is a woman wishing for epiphany as she tries to train her brain, which needs remedial obedience school and has the reflexes of a fat old dachshund. The tattoo artist tells you of her fascination with Joseph Cornell and his boxes.

———————

I came back to *no further* in a roundabout way, as I sat in my car in the parking lot of the Department of Natural Resources at Ohio State, just about to get out and walk through a small arboretum, seeking quiet.

It felt very Minneapolis, very down-to-the-bone and what-next, one of those times where I needed to find a coffee shop job and start building a new life. I have always loved the names of cities. During a jewelry-making class in Chicago, I used a set of letter stamps and a mallet to pound the names of places where

I'd loved or lived onto strips of copper, then strung them on a crude necklace: Boston, Berlin, Marl, Chicago, Minneapolis, Subiaco. I wore the necklace, reminding myself that I'd been through so many coffee shops and on so many exit ramps, had located so many post offices, and that I was good at finding the library and the best place to buy notebooks and bread.

Minneapolis led to all those memories, led to the bridge, and so I went back to my office at work and entered my phrase from the long-ago poem into a search engine. I kept clicking and dreading that after fourteen years, my little sentence would be revealed to be random or meaningless. Ten more minutes led me to the author, then the poem. Now, a decade later, you can find it easily by searching for my mantra.

Imagine you are standing above a highway, walking slowly, and that you move as each word is revealed. Imagine a Minneapolis wind that whips the clouds, and imagine that the lights of the city to the northeast are just winking on in amber and yellow. Imagine metal behind each letter, that a large piece of architecture forces you into patience and a creeping slowness. The entire poem begins with a place of "old order / But the tail end of the movement is new / Driving us to say what we are thinking." Ashbery puts me on a beach, and then I find my mantra. It makes a tight sense. I count the lines: eight above and eight below my special sentence. It is surrounded with octave eights, an infinite loop, like walking the bridge back and forth, the space in the middle a place to rest and to return to. "This far, it is fair to be crossing, to have crossed." I am soothed to know that by accident, raw and twenty, I inadvertently found the center.

MY MEN (REPRISE)

In the express checkout line of a local grocery store in Columbus, Ohio, a guy in line ahead of me started to pay for a twenty-ounce Sam Adams, and the clerk asked for his ID.

"Figures I would get carded tonight. I'm turning thirty tomorrow."

I overheard him and laughed. He looked back at me, this wiry guy dressed in a black T-shirt, jeans, and a flannel shirt. His Motörhead baseball cap was pulled down low over his eyebrows. His narrow face broke into a smile, and wrinkles bloomed at the outer corners of his eyes.

"At least you have a beard," I said. I was twenty-nine but had been told I looked like a sophisticated thirteen.

"I'm a Scorpio, born in '69," he said. "It's the last night of my twenties."

I blushed for this punk-rock alterna-boy. I knew I looked like a fourth-grader in my old plaid coat and a sweater. His eyes were darkish and intense but friendly, not hey-baby manipulative.

I walked home with my groceries, and he pulled up beside me in a car covered with dull, tan-gray primer and skateboarding stickers. Extension cords, the dark plastic faces of power tools, and pieces of wood were heaped in the back. He leaned over the front seat to roll down the window.

"Do you want a ride?" His smile was genuine, and his voice had a nervous upswing at the end. "I mean, you probably think I'm a psycho or a stalker, but I was just driving by and I saw you."

He seemed nice and all, but I didn't have a death wish. "No, but thanks." I smiled and stuck my hand in the car to introduce myself. I learned his name, Abe, and we figured out we lived two blocks apart. At home, I lay on the couch and held my breath, wondering.

Five days later, I stepped into the express checkout aisle at 9:00 p.m. with a *Glamour* magazine, a bag of instant salad, and some orange juice. Abe stood in front of me, paying for a banana and a chocolate muffin.

"Hey," I said.

He turned around, looked at me in shock, and laughed. "I guess this means I'm supposed to give you my number," he said.

I walked with him down the hill from the grocery store toward our apartments. We figured out, during the three-minute walk, that we both liked punk rock and loved coffee, enough excuses for us to hang out.

Abe asked if I wanted to see his apartment, and I said sure. His cats came rushing toward the open door, faces pressed into the widening crack, and we maneuvered around them into the narrow kitchen. One open kitchen wall was painted, covered from floor to ceiling with looping lines in yellow, dark blue, turquoise, brown, and green. Down the narrow hallway hung two paintings on scrap wood and cardboard, and the living room was filled with art made from skateboards, polished turned wood, and twisted metal, massive gray and black and red and white abstract paintings, all carefully composed to make the small space into a rebel gallery. I have replayed these moments in my mind for decades since, wondering if it was possible not to fall, watching myself teetering on the edge.

I am a first-generation middle-class daughter of an immigrant and a first-generation American. People like me walk the fine line between fucked and fine.

My mother once said, in a single conversation, "You don't need money to have a good life. You just need family," and "I want you to marry the editor of the *Chicago Sun-Times*." She chose the city's working-class South Side paper as my final destination rather than the larger, iconic *Tribune*. Maybe it seemed more doable. She just wants me to be deeply, truly happy, I thought, which would ideally include being free from the money stress that turned her, at one point, into a three-pack-a-day smoker.

Around that time, I did sit on the couch some days, overcome with a strong but shadowy guilt. I wasn't making enough or saving enough to erase those money worries, and it seemed like I wouldn't marry "up," the unstated responsibility to pair with someone who owned an expensive college degree. Marrying "over and out" to different emotional ranges, different ways of being, has driven me more furiously. I also keep coming back to men who are shades of the rawer men I have known.

Sometime between when I was seven and ten, my mom found a Barbie penthouse at a garage sale, and we set it up on the back porch. I remember standing Barbie and Ken in the top floor of the four-story structure. Ken was barefoot because my sister and I kept losing his shoes. We didn't bother putting together outfits for him at all, so he had to wear a homemade sweater my mom knitted and a pair of garage-sale brown pants someone else's mom had sewn.

The penthouse's cardboard walls were decorated in a seventies theme, a room in pinks and blues to match the pink plastic pillars supporting the roof. Looking into the pasted pictures of windows on the walls revealed a city at night, the skyline's red and white and yellow lights in the blue distance. I squinted to make those painted city lights twinkle, standing on our back porch on the edge of a cornfield in summer with scraped knees and purple cutoff shorts.

My first two college boyfriends were both from wealthy New York families, and their appeal had something to do with that Barbie moment, of being up high in a city apartment at night with a clear stretch of glass and a view of the traffic moving below. One boyfriend took me to the summer home of a wealthy family friend, and I broke a fancy teak patio chair by sitting on it wrong. Later, over dinner, the hosts asked me questions about myself and my plans. When I blushed and stumbled, they laughed good-naturedly and lectured me about how being shy would not help me get ahead in life. I went outside and fell asleep on a warm rock next to their tennis court, wishing myself dead. At dinners with both these boys' families, I felt my lack of polish like a blank space between my eyes. I could watch myself from the inside out, know how my expressions, the things I did with my hands and my mouth, and the way I sat on my hands to prevent myself from waving them around while I spoke all marked me as a dangerous, foolhardy choice for these carefully raised sons.

My men can get degrees, but they can slip back into the fold if they buy tools and stock the workshops of suburban homes. As long as they buy a Ford F-150, even if it's souped up, the door opens both ways for them. They become invisible, and the coasts read this place in a monotone white cartoon. Reagan, an Illinois son, went coastal and came back as a right-wing maniac to gut the unions that once gave my men a regular paycheck. But the white cutout hides us all, from others and from ourselves; the Midwest is home to more Black people than New England or the West, writes Tamara Winfrey-Harris, and Daisy Hernández describes the region as Latin American.[1] Its reality, and its past, is in process, becoming.

Abe took me for a ride in his '72 Dodge Dart, gunning the motor around twisting on-ramps beneath the pale fall sun and the city's short, stocky skyline. He told me about his dead father as we drank coffee, and I watched the side of his face, waiting for bitterness or arrogance to cloud the patient light in his eyes. He took me to a place he said was an ancient Indigenous burial mound, behind which was a chain link fence and beyond it, a reservoir. We watched the crows above the water and talked about our families, about siblings and parents and nightmare scenes, and how it all looked snarled and unfinished from a distance.

I told him I couldn't get into a relationship and knew when I said it that I was lying. After Thanksgiving, we kissed on the front porch and then stumbled for the couch, where we stayed until 3:00 a.m. The next day, he went up to the grocery store, found the checkout clerk who'd been ringing out our groceries when we met, and told this stranger what a cool thing had begun near his register.

1 Tamara Winfrey-Harris, "Stop Pretending Black Midwesterners Don't Exist," *New York Times*, June 16, 2018; Daisy Hernández, "How the Midwest is Latin American," *National Geographic*, May 3, 2022.

A week later, Abe sat on my bed after pulling off his sweatshirt, wearing a sleeveless undershirt that exposed a thin muscled torso, the heartbreaking bulge of shoulders, defined biceps like trapped potential energy. A tattooed portrait of his dead father's face, eerily photo-realistic, stared out from his left upper arm.

"I look like total white trash to you, I bet," he said, eyebrows cocked at me. "Tattoos and a wifebeater." He watched me with half a laugh, and I groaned.

"God, I hate that word," I said. I was talking about his use of "wifebeater" for his sleeveless ribbed T-shirt. And I had no lecture ready for the phrase "white trash," a familiar epithet that stung with judgment but seemed also to illuminate a complicated and familiar anxiety. The expression of that anxiety or awareness made me relax, somehow, let me know he understood things that so many people in my life did not.

He laughed nervously. "I don't know why I said it," he said. "I wanted to say it to see what you would say. It's what the skaters call it, anyway."

I know why he said it—to test me, learn the rules.

"Are you a wifebeater, just because you wear that?"

He fell onto his back, grabbed the striped comforter, and pulled it into a ball to cover his face, muffle his voice. "Damn, you're so correct about everything, and I feel like everything I say is wrong."

My stomach muscles clenched up, and I was torn between speaking my mind as a woman and shutting up as a bratty college kid. I could relate to his "everything I say is wrong." I swore way too much in class, and I talked with my hands, feeling raw and dirty and hard. Then I heard Abe praising his lucky stars at this "educated princess" he'd snagged. Or I went home to my family, and a few fancy words fell out of my mouth, and I felt prissy and overintellectual—a stuck-up scrub, a smart hick.

My brother's wedding took place in the tiny town of Sterling, Illinois, a few weeks before my encounters with Abe in the grocery store. It was in late October, and I came without a date. After the reception hall tossed us out, we crowded into a sports bar at the Holiday Inn. In the middle of a shouted conversation, some wrong word came out of my mouth. I don't even remember what it was and didn't notice that I'd done it. I only know that it was a few too many syllables, something to mark me as a book person. The kidding started, jokes about how smart I thought I was, how it was time to study for the SAT. Because I was drunk, tears sprang to my eyes. I was the first woman from both sides of my family to ever go to college who did not have to become a nun to get there.

John, my brother's best man, put a baseball cap advertising a brand of cattle feed on my head and hugged me to him. Somebody yelled for more beer.

"Yeah, I bet you think I'm a winner, huh? I go to DeVry Technical Institute," laughed another groomsman.

John added, "We're pretty much winners—we both still live with our moms."

It felt more urgent than a joke. I was not a person but an instrument for measuring achievement in reverse. The jokes always felt like preemptive attacks against being judged, attempts to draw me in and push me away, responses to something I gave off, a part of myself that I held away from them, my futile and long-nourished hopes of being special.

I was voted "most likely to succeed" in high school. In those photos, which I still think about sometimes, the yearbook photographer posed my mathlete friend Mike and me next to a teacher's old Cadillac in the parking lot, with our noses in the air and our fingertips holding them aloft, the universal signal for "stuck up." To succeed is to become arrogant, to betray, to become unmoored.

———————

In December, Abe stopped over for coffee, straight from work, smelling like cut wood. He walked in and held me, then toured the apartment, covered it with his eyes. He stopped in front of the floor-to-ceiling bookshelves, scanned the book spines, his eyes glancing off the titles. He stood below a poster from a strike of newspaper workers in Detroit, walked past the windowsill that held my piles of rocks and seed pods and glass bottles. Maybe he checked out my sorry housekeeping, the dust in the corners and the dull floors, the empty coffee cups guarding every flat surface like pigeons on a sidewalk.

We sat on the couch and talked. He picked at the end of his callused thumb with a safety pin. He dislodged a splinter, which shot out of his thumb one-eighth of an inch, driven by pus and the force of infection. There were splinters all over his hands, waiting their turn to bust free through the crust of his calluses. He looked up at me, catching my fascination with the process of extracting wood from his body.

"The salesmen, the guys at the front, they don't know shit—don't know how to read a tape measure. They should double-check their measurements, but they don't." Abe worked at a roaring factory, complete with bells and a punch clock, with 180 employees, mostly Russians and Somalis. He started his day at 6:30 a.m., putting together special-order paneled doors out of cherry, mahogany, walnut, and other expensive hardwoods.

That day, a team of three managers had come back to the special-order area, waited for him to pull out his earplugs, take off his safety glasses, and turn off his saw. They yelled at him because an irate customer had received double eight-foot mahogany doors that didn't fit their frame. Abe dug out the work order, he told me, and found the error—the salesman's quarter-of-an-inch mistake, which in the language of doors is a chasm.

"White-collar boneheads. It's so easy for them to assume I don't know anything, that it's me who made the mistake."

A six-hour drive to New Lenox, an hour south of Chicago, landed Abe and me in my parents' kitchen, 10:00 on a Friday night, road-dazed and nervous, trying out the feeling of playing a couple in front of my oldest audience. My mom served pork chops, and my brother told us about the sump pump backing up, about going outside in the freezing rain to take apart a valve. He was chewing tobacco more furiously than normal since he'd given up smoking again. He spit his tobacco juice into an empty pop can, talking with a half-lisp around the bulge in his lower lip. He was plaid-jacketed, over six feet tall, and surly with a day's scruff of beard. His steel-toed black leather boots balanced on stool rungs.

"You can't use that valve in the winter," my mom explained to my brother, telling him how to fix the pump. "The water freezes up and seals the valve, so you get a flood when water hits the ice. Take that off until the summer," she said. She drew the pump in the air with her hands. She is a short, round German woman with bright eyes who lives exclusively on butter, potatoes, and various meats. She is the decision-maker, the compass of the house, a smiling bulldog.

My dad, not a talker or a bonder, sat with Abe at the counter and made small talk. He disappeared for a moment, then returned with a paperweight he made in college: a real cat brain with the eyeballs still attached, back from when he was studying biology and still thought he might be able to go to medical school.

Dad ran his finger along the underside of the paperweight, showed Abe where you once could see the optic nerve. Now the brain was a gray lump, with ghostly points where the pupils were still visible in the orbs of the eyes.

Abe held the paperweight, probably thinking about his two beloved cats, and looked at me for half a second: *What the fuck?* Then he handed it back, and my dad turned the conversation over to a job he'd had during that time, working as an attendant on the geriatric ward of a hospital, another part of his medical school bid that went awry. Dad was giving of himself and his life story to a stranger, to a man I had just brought into the house. The quick show-and-tell for Abe was more personal information than I'd gotten from Dad in the last five years put together.

Abe saw right away that his princess estimation of me was half right. I felt it in the first scan he took of the house, taking in the knickknacks and the antique clocks and the new couches my mom had just ordered. It was certainly not a castle, but it was a two-income household, where there had been regular vacations and three kids sent to college.

"Your mom is a little badass," he said later, as we lay in bed in my room. "I like your Dad, he's like a big teddy bear." My family members would have laughed at that characterization, but maybe we see Dad through a haze of the tense and stressed man he was years ago. "I like the way he talks," Abe added, catching my Dad's Arkansas drawl. Abe felt it too, the hesitant reaching of my Dad's heart out of its shell toward him.

———————

I sat on Abe's black and white couch on a Saturday morning in August, my legs twined up with his. He stretched across the couch, his head against the armrest. We were fueled with sleep, morning sex, and coffee. We unloaded the stresses in our lives to each other. His job had aggravated an old back injury that left him bent and squinting, breathing hard. He wanted to find something better for more money, "because if you want a house, kids, all that stuff, it's hard to do on $9.50 an hour." I was looking for work after grad school, unable to get hired either as a reporter or a receptionist, wishing the city had more jobs that wanted me.

We unfolded ourselves, and I walked out the screen door to stand in the sunshine on Abe's front porch and check the progress of his puttied and primed and sanded Dodge Dart. He leaned out the kitchen door, calling for his cats, shirtless, wearing ripped army pant cutoffs, thick-soled black skateboard shoes, and a yellow and green mesh baseball cap with a red and black patch that said "Independent." He rested his forearms on the cap of his blue Toyota pickup truck, which was backed up against the cement stoop, and picked blue and orange paint from his fingernails, traces of his latest art project. He held a small cellophane bag at me.

"You want some beef jerky?"

"Excellent," I said. "Been a long time."

He looked at me for two or three seconds, just resting his eyes on mine.

"I knew you'd like beef jerky. Man, that's fucking cool."

He smiled at me with obvious pride, the same look I got when I told him to fuck off and he deserved it, when I told him he was being sexist, when I pulled a nail from the garbage disposal in his sink, when I lugged heavy boxes out to my pickup truck. It is easy to get approval from men for a pout, for a piece of hair falling in front of the face, for a short skirt. It is harder to feel loved for being tough without being hard.

"I eat it at work," he said. "I put some in between my lip and teeth like tobacco chew."

The taste of nostalgia is salty and smoked, and it smells like a hot day that softens and heats the vinyl seat of an old car, with a man inside in a thin white T-shirt clutching a golden can of Miller High Life, the champagne of beers. What are you longing for? That silent afternoon when nobody was worried to death, and you were there, laughing. And under that glistening, thin wrapping of the imagined past is something new, a place where you can breathe.

GLASS BEADS

In the green fake-velvet jewelry box I got sometime in high school, I keep two smooth blobs of glass about the size of grapes. They rest heavily in my palm and make tiny *tik-tik* noises when their surfaces touch.

The clear glass of one captures a crumpled swirl of blue. The other freezes a looping whirl of red. When these blobs of glass were heated to a near-liquid state, glowing dully, their surface tension dropped. You folded each top down into its body, making a loop for stringing a cord.

The fact that you made me two beads is touching, even now. When you gave them to me, I held them in my palm to admire them. I strung both of them on a long silver chain, but they bunched together strangely, jabbing my sternum when I held a book or laundry basket to my chest. I took off the blue one and left just the red, but I never really liked how it looked. It didn't look right because I knew it wasn't just a bead.

It was as though the beads had been dipped in an invisible coating of grime. I knew you experimented with glassblowing while building tables at a studio, and you told me that the glassblowing set-up was used to create elaborate pipes and bongs in lovely ropes of starburst colors.

I had always loved the idea of glassblowing, and my family visited a glass factory when my brother, sister, and I were young—the glassblowers who made cranberry glass in West Virginia—and it was beautiful and fantastic to watch the glow that swirled and morphed sluggishly against the drag and torque of spinning, the way the surface bloomed and captured motion as it cooled. I loved the way dirty, smudged hands could create an utterly smooth and mirrored surface with sand and heat. The most graceful art, I thought.

But then I cringed to see a row of pipes in a head shop, glass blown not for the art but for function, in cheesy color combinations like children's balloons. It made me resent these glassblowers. They have a right to do whatever they want with their free time, and the art of glassblowing is still beautiful. Why did I care? It was jealousy, I think—the way you craved and smiled at and stroked a new pipe, the sheer fondness you had for it. You never got irritated or angry at a pipe. You never blamed a pipe for anything. The world was never the fault of the pipe or the bong.

I love beads. I collect them and string them, making necklaces and earrings and taking them apart. I like surprising combinations, and I love their durability and their pointlessness, only they are not pointless. On dark days, I would loop a string of confetti-colored beads around my neck, and that yoke of sun would maybe make a cashier smile and say, "I like your necklace," and then I would smile and say thank you and feel less alone. Beads are like flowers. They draw human contact. And in the mirror, the thin, breakable strings that held them together remind me to fake it or to reach, to string my own energy and words and sentences and desires just a touch farther than I feel I can.

Those two beads were blown in a studio stocked with tools you touched. The tools were also touched by another man and his brother, both of them embroiled in the city's marijuana trade.

Those brothers bragged to you that they had murdered someone who didn't pay his drug debt. And then there was a kid missing, and he made the news because he was a white college student. And you said, "That was him," your eyes semiwide as if you didn't know what to do with this information but were telling me not to tell anyone. You weren't scared, of course, because you're safe if you stay on the same side as the murderers.

At the time, I was so stunned that I didn't know what to do with this information linked to a dead young man. At the time, I knew the dealer's last name. It is here: _____. Trapped in my head, in glass, along with a few details about where one of the brothers used to work.

And I did the worst thing imaginable. I compartmentalized the information, put it away as a cold nugget I could do nothing with, like the glass beads that were too heavy and big to wear.

Later, I thought a lot about a body that was supposed to have been left in a ditch near a cornfield. I read and searched for news articles about the missing young man. I think I kept seeking them out because I was trying to remind myself this was real. Or maybe the two brothers were talking shit. Or maybe they told you a story you heard wrong. Maybe it was someone else who told them that story. But you said they were dangerous.

It was like I swallowed those cold beads. I wanted to throw them away but I could not do it. They were the last link I had to something of critical importance. But I did nothing, as if the connections between you and these murderers were a white-hot bar heated in a furnace that would burn my hands. I could have picked up the phone, I supposed, though the homicide police had a tip line and were overloaded with information. Maybe someone else had already reported the murder.

Now the name is a space in my head I cannot excavate.

Then another young man—your friend, the one who introduced you to these dangerous characters, the one who went to jail and stunned us every day by still being alive and smiling his goofy smile, the one who had a tattoo on his neck of two pigs fucking—overdosed and exploded his heart in a hotel room. There was no funeral. You organized a memorial service in a park. It was small and punctuated with laughter and the sounds of children playing on the swing set. The crack-addled and the crack-recovered and you and I came to pay our respects, and we cried.

Years later, I searched online for the name of the murdered young man and found out his parents were still looking for him. I used that city's anonymous tip website and wrote down everything I knew. I don't know if anything happened. I never heard back from the police.

When my students mention lamp work or blowing glass with a laugh—"Ha ha, I made the most excellent bong or pipe"—I want to throw up. I drive by the head shop in town and my heart dips. I want to throw away those two glass beads, but I make myself keep them. They are in my jewelry box, and I will never throw them away. They are my anonymous memorial to the boy who disappeared and to my own cowardice, confusion, and denial.

GOAT-BABY

It is the end of May, and the goat-baby (the bubble, the little being—all these nicknames to help us both be fond yet keep our distance) is eleven weeks old. It has finally closed whatever valves and soaked up whatever potions were making the room tip; the peanut was raining poppy dust in my veins and making me sleep at inconvenient times. The fetus is willful and at peak intelligence before it ever speaks. Maybe we are already resisting each other.

I dipped into my previous life this morning, swallowed lovely brown coffee and jumped off the bridge of tiredness down into the traffic of words. The computer's square screen made me stare, and I forgot to eat or go to the bathroom. I squinted for a second and looked up to see that an hour had passed. A revered fiction teacher's mantra played in my head: "Kill your darlings." Two and a half feet down from this scary brain is a defenseless flesh-comma. I don't think I look like a mommy, hunched over my computer screen with a scowl, biting at my lips and my nails.

I lose myself in my work, then I worry I've been cheating. Have I somehow made myself unpregnant, broken the shallow membrane between my hopes and the multiple worlds in my head? If I stop thinking about the baby, does it die? If I leave my body for lines of text, who reminds the baby's cells to divide, and who keeps it from getting lonely?

It's week sixteen. Happy sweet sixteen, goat-baby. I promise I'll stop calling you goat when we find out next month what you are. Goat-baby, I love you so much, but I'm glad you're not here yet. Rather than counting down the weeks, I am banking against them, hoping for the full forty.

In the coffee shop, I met with an accomplished writer who's also the mother of an eight-year-old. "Look, you can do it," she said as she glanced down at her watch, timing the minutes until she had to go pick up her daughter. "Just make sure you have a draft of the book done before the baby comes. You think you'll have time afterward, and people always say, 'Oh, I'll write when the baby sleeps,' but that's bullshit. You're going to be sleeping or staring at the baby. So get to work and have the most productive summer of your life."

When friends ask me how I'm doing, I am honest only if I know them well. I say, "I'm panicked. I haven't ever had this kind of a deadline before." To one friend, who is also a writer thinking about getting pregnant this year, I say, "You know, it feels like somehow December 2 is the date I'm going to die." Then the disclaimers: "I mean, I know that's sick, and of course, I don't really think that . . ."

She nods. "I know exactly what you mean. It's like, goodbye to everything."

It's a sick metaphor—of course, it's the opposite of a death. It's something the mommy on the cover of the pregnancy manual would never say or even think.

I've heard the urge for domestic completion described as a nesting instinct, a burst of furious activity before giving birth. I'm writing today in an office that's going to become your bedroom, while my future writing space waits: a tiny alcove off the bedroom, just big enough for a desk. When we looked at our limited floor plan and figured out the allotment of rooms, I had an undignified hormonal crash and spent an afternoon crying about it. When I got up and washed off my face, I felt selfish and confused; I thought the maternal instinct would suck all of those feelings away like poison from a snakebite.

So this will become your nest, but there's no sign of a nursery. It's disgusting, actually: paper everywhere, some of it in drifts. It's hard to tell this room isn't rounded at the bottom like a bowl. That corner is the classes I'll be teaching; this half of the desk and the floor below it is the book; behind me is the political work I won't have time for anymore . . .

I wonder if I'm embezzling from my maternal wellspring, burning the energy that is supposed to be used for picking out wallpaper with bunnies and lambs.

I am happy for the blood barrier of the placenta that keeps some of my fluids separate from yours, because my mental soup is no place for a baby. I know you will develop tastes for what I ate during pregnancy. You can have buckets of chicken tikka masala if you want.

While my belly reaches outward, my brain and my hands—held so close to my lap—are trying to write a book about the rise of the Third Reich, about fascism, that will mirror our homegrown surge when you are a teenager. Sweetheart, I hope you never read this and figure out I spent your gestation trying to close the empathy gap and feel the fear that a German Marxist had in his throat for Hitler's brownshirts. I'm sorry if you sensed my fear.

For selfish me, I want my work. For you, sometimes it seems much better and kinder to have a mommy like the one on the cover of *What to Expect When You're Expecting*, the book I grew to loathe and called *Mothering, Incorporated*. It seemed to have no guidance for the challenges I encountered.

At week twenty-one, a friend told me about a thrift store for maternity and baby clothes. Today, browsing the aisles and piling up three-dollar shorts and five-dollar dresses, pausing in front of a huge bin filled with tiny socks, I felt temporarily at rest. Moms flipped through T-shirts and piloted strollers through the aisles, and a clenching within my chest released its tightened spring. Welcome to thrifting, baby. I hope you like the pride of something twice-used and comfortably broken in.

Shyly touching a Winnie-the-Pooh lamp, a cute swirl of color I didn't think I'd ever be able to afford, I felt the edges of a real life open up for us. Your dad and mom are both artists, making our living as "freelancers." We have flexible schedules and decidedly unimpressive incomes. You will know, as we know, the wonders of the Dollar Store, the binges at the library. I knew this—I knew all along this was how it would be.

Hanging my brand-name, slightly used dresses on hangers, I realized I've been so intimidated by you, baby. I had this weird idea you were going to pop out of me judging and dissatisfied, like a prefab suburban child expecting a stay-at-home mom and a Lexus SUV to take her to playgroup. I have been already ducking in shame, imagining the sneer in your liquid brown eyes when you bury your face in a receiving blanket and come up for air with the distinctive smell and imprint on your face, knowing this blankie is garage-sale worn.

"It's twice-loved, baby. And it was only a dollar," I would say. But you'd already be hating me, already be following the North Star of your compass, waiting to escape to the life you knew you came here for, the life every Gerber baby was promised.

The thrift store—real, concrete, with helpful and harried women behind the counter, not ashamed to be pushing the economical and the shared—made me realize, with a surge of greedy pride and calculation, that we will get you first. Before your little consciousness is even formed to narrow your eyes at Daddy's backyard full of sculptures and at Mommy's chaotic office, you will be spoiled with rescued treasures, homemade toys, and the best games and on-the-spot stories two parents can invent. If we can't give you the moon and can't guarantee you much saved for college, we can at least show you the wide world, the one that exists beyond traditional opportunity. You are not even a five-month-old fetus, and you've already come along to ten demonstrations and felt the sun outside your warm womb at a New York beach where tattooed gay boys romped naked in the waves. You will be loved but never shackled with the blinders that make real life seem frightening.

We bought your baby book on clearance, dear. It's a blank journal with a beaded cover. The pictures and collages and memories and stories that will go inside will, you can be sure, be yours alone.

Walking near the river in the evening tonight, watching a two-year-old getting pushed on a swing and tipping his head back in ecstasy, in flagrant display of his own personality, I was thinking about you and the ways you will have. We will see your twenty-one-week-old body tomorrow in ghostly grays on the ultrasound screen, and we will learn only hints about you, but I am hungry for every clue: any arch of an eyebrow or curve of a foot will be outrageous and specific. In this moment, my curiosity has eclipsed my anxiety.

My skin is expanding around you, and it's interesting but not entirely unfamiliar to be inhabited by a strange character, to think about the spaces inside me that I don't own. This stage feels like the prewriting of a story: that tentative, intuitive brooding. I flip through gestures and looks, not searching for a composite but for someone I want to understand.

Writing is the only way to replicate the feeling and privilege of being in love; those are the only two moments when staring is not impolite, when we are allowed to revel in the skin-landscape, the minute gestures, the smell and dastardly contradictions of another person. Last time we saw you, you were soap bubbles, semitransparent globes scattered around a hummingbird's beating heart. I want to see you; I am hungry for the plot, for the tiny details of your story contained in the pads of your fingers and your plans for future rebellion.

GREETINGS FROM DIVORCELAND!

You eye that ride for a year or three. You want the raging rush and breathless triple-loop of change, but the tracks lead straight to Super-Single-Mother Swamp. The ride will leave you out there on that spooky island by yourself, with family, help, and ex-husband an eleven-hour drive away.

You take the plunge, and once you recover from the tinny waves of jet-lag exhaustion, you boost your cell phone minutes and start taking vitamins again. You're on this ride alone with your boy, who seems charmed by the rushing and the curves. You talk in a low murmur through the ride, tell him what each painted backdrop means. *Look*, you say, *there's Obama—his mommy was a single parent too.* The whipping of the car snatches at mittens and soccer practice schedules, and Good-Enough-Mom looms above you. E-mails and messages are brief and pointed because you're traveling at high speeds and can only get out a few stretched and shouted words as you pass. Rehearse the souvenirs of your mortality, the reminders of the good person you used to be.

Look ahead to the twists and turns: long stretches of unbroken childrearing will bring a kind of exhausted, athletic delight. You can't see beyond the bend. You don't yet know that one load of laundry shared in scorekeeping bitterness is much heavier than two lifted with simple joy. You will need sleep, and you dredge up the warnings you never heeded from your son's infancy. Sleep when the baby sleeps. You worry about that scattered, sick-day, single-mother stereotype. There will be those days.

Beyond the last curve, you slow to the island and see the waterfall and pools of relief you hadn't dared dream about. Time is scarce here, but happiness and relief turn the time into another substance entirely. Your skin absorbs the wet silence, and you know it will be easier to mother in this particular wilderness.

Plan the redecorating trip to Ikea. Buy your forbidden foods: tofu, beets, soy milk. Take down the picture of motorcycles in the hall and throw away the towels in your soon-to-be-ex-mother-in-law's favorite color, a bashful mossy gray-green. Buy a box of postdivorce condoms, wipe clean the counters, and throw away the menus from the compromise restaurants along with the hated knickknacks and the dollar-store bubble bath.

Out on this island, feel your body as solid, yours, not leased to the outside world but of the world, licked by oak leaves and maple-seed helicopters. You didn't imagine the bridges, cities, and roads. You gas up your dented Sentra and head to visit the relatives and friends who hug you long and hard. You are fully owned by whatever stretch of the highway you are driving through as you hand another Fruit Roll-Up to your boy in the back seat. Welcome to your date with lonely, wistful, complicated, demanding-yet-affectionate today; hello, beloved open-ended silence and surprise. Stay here among the living, past the illusions of ownership.

BREASTFEEDING DICK CHENEY

1.

It's difficult to describe my relationship with Dick Cheney—even now, after all this time. We share a birthday, January 30, though I was born thirty years after him. Both the eldest of three children, we were talkative kids and avid readers. Our parents each drove all over the country on long, low-budget road trips. He was raised by Democrat parents and turned, as I turned against my Republican parents. Our trips to elite private colleges led to panic and homesickness. We have dealt with our anxiety issues in opposite ways. We have struggled with codependence—that feeling of our identity being subsumed into another person's. I've tried to get over mine. Dick has made his a way of life.

I will not assume you share my feelings toward Dick Cheney, but I will assume there is a person on the globe who raises your hackles, whose misuse of power troubles your heart. Please believe me: this is not directly about politics. It is about that fearsome wave of hate. The only strangers here are those who would deny having such feelings.

2.

I am a midwesterner with a Middle Eastern shadow. I belong to the Middle Eastern generation, bookended and contained by the conflict that my country launched. My childhood carries the echo of the word "Shah," the hostage crisis, then the Gulf War in college, the 576,000 dead Iraq children in the economic embargo, and then another war.[1] In the dark, I cast my mind across the oceans to Iraq, to Persia, to Babylon. Heat rises in the pink of my eyelids and my esophagus. My mom was born in Germany after World War II and says she owes her life to the Marshall Plan that funded the country's reconstruction, so I have a bias that favors rebuilding after bombing and the ousting of dictators. I Google "rebuild Iraq" but don't know who to donate to. Iraq has probably had just about enough of people like me wanting to help.

Cheney agrees about the fixation: "We're always going to have to be involved [in the Middle East]. Maybe it's part of our national character, you know we like to have these problems nice and neatly wrapped up, put a ribbon around it . . . it doesn't work that way in the Middle East it never has and isn't likely to in my lifetime."[2]

3.

I got pregnant about a month after President George W. Bush uttered the fateful sixteen words in his January 28, 2003, State of the Union address: "The British government has learned that Saddam Hussein recently sought significant quantities of uranium from Africa." Cheney pushed the connection between 9/11 and Iraq and personally brought evidence to the CIA.[3] I spent the couch days of morning sickness watching the war unfold, watching this man who duck-talked through a mouth slotted like a crooked piggy bank.

I made chocolate cake for my son's first birthday in 2004. He's had six war birthdays since then, and now he doesn't like

1 Barbara Crossette, "Iraq Sanctions Kill Children, UN Reports," *New York Times*, Dec. 1, 1995.
2 "Oral History: Dick Cheney," *Frontline*, Public Broadcasting System, http://www.pbs.org/wgbh/pages/front-line/gulf/oral/cheney/2.html.
3 Thomas Powers, "What George Tenet Really Knew about Iraq," *Salon*, July 2, 2007.

chocolate. In the grocery aisle, I stop in front of the icings and cake mixes. I reach for a box of Duncan Hines and wonder if maybe this year he will turn back to chocolate.

I can't make myself buy yellow cake. In the shadows of my mind, the sunshine substance is linked to yellowcake uranium, which Hussein supposedly purchased, though that was based on a lie or on mistaken Nigerian intelligence Cheney touted. For one birthday, my son insisted on yellow, and the lumpy toxic look of it in the bowl made me nauseous. I usually buy white cake mix with multicolored confetti sprinkles.

4.

I visited a Buddhist temple in Columbus, Ohio, for the first time in spring 2004, overwhelmed with bitterness. I had read about a meditation practice to cultivate *bodhichitta*, love for all beings. Another practice, *tonglen*, asks you to imagine someone you don't like and then to breathe in all pain while breathing out peace and happiness for them.

I imagined a map of the country and the world, but with burn marks like cigarette scars to fit neatly around certain people. All beings: that is the part that makes your brain frazzled. If you haven't tried it, feeling love for Dick Cheney creates heartburn and a headache. Your brain has to develop four-wheel drive to handle the terrain, and this is all you notice: neurons busting out of their tracks.

I clutch my Cheney-hatred like a teddy bear. I worry that if I don't hate him, somehow, someone will forget what he's done. But I am not a lighthouse, and I have to learn to trust the world. It's all written down; we bear it together. In dropping my Cheney-hatred for one minute, I free-fall. I don't know who I am without it. He is the star I navigate against.

Cheney had his first of five heart attacks in 1978. With the mention of his recent heart difficulties, I pause. I imagine being able to reach into his chest and jostle it.[4] Others share the horrifying, delicious thought.[5] I want to lift off my sternum to examine my hate, pick it out, and force myself to understand it. This murderous thought is the dream of terrorists, assassins, and children. My Cheney problem is a child's story. Dehumanization is the quickest way to turn bodies into fuel. Maybe we know we will have to use these simple ideas to keep us warm when the oil runs out.

Heat any substance to around 470 degrees Celsius and it will start to glow, which is known as incandescence. Light and heat are released, along with gases that combine with the oxygen and carbon dioxide in the atmosphere. The heat keeps the fuel hot, which releases more gases and makes more fire. The word "incandescent" also means "a person who is wound up to a sustained white heat of anger." My Cheney problem is an incandescent light bulb of hatred.

Do I have a right to be angry? I am an American, and it takes so much oil to fuel my anger. I hear the heater roaring in the background. I have a load of clothes in the washing machine. I will take a hot water shower. I type on a glowing monitor. The internet blazes with the secondary incandescence of trapped energy. Whenever I see electricity in motion, I think of Iraq. What is the by-product? What work is being done in the light of this fire? What is the size of Dick Cheney's carbon footprint?

4 This murderous urge comes from the waste of Cheney's war. Even conservative think tanks such as the Cato Institute declared before the war, "Iraq does not represent a threat to American national security. In fact, invading and occupying Iraq will likely undermine American national security, perhaps catastrophically so." G. Healy, "Iraq: Wrong Place, Wrong Time, Wrong War," *Cato Institute*, Jan. 1, 2003. Before the invasion, Cheney held meetings to iron out how to "jump-start Iraq's oil industry after a war." Thaddeus Herrick, "U.S. Wants to Work in Iraq," in *Wall Street Journal*, Jan. 16, 2003, via "About Halliburton: Halliburton/Cheney Chronology," *Halliburton Watch*.

5 Ken Layne, "Waiting for Dick Cheney to Die? Get a Chair," *Wonkette*, June 26, 2010.

5.

Iraq leaked into my writing classes in rural southeast Georgia. I told my hunting, camo-wearing, mostly Baptist students this wasn't about politics. It was about the Middle East in our heads, about the arguments at the bars and frat parties. Nobody complained; no irate parents called. I handed out a blank hand-drawn map of the Middle East.

"Name the countries," I said.

The students failed, mouths agape.

"This isn't going to count toward our grades, is it?"

I told them no; I made the quiz, and I failed it too. We learned that there were downtowns and McDonalds in Middle Eastern cities, that kids wore jeans and wanted to dance. We aimed for humanization, so I had to look back at my own brain.

6.

Advanced Buddhist monks sometimes hang out in graveyards or stare at dead bodies or think of themselves decaying, which is called "charnal ground" meditation—all to confront the brain with its own lack of control.

I found a new meditation teacher, Dzigar Kongtrul Rinpoche, at the end of 2009 and began a year of preparation to become his formal student. He assigned four basic scenarios, versions of Buddhist compassion visualizations that have been used for millennia. The point isn't to walk around feeling special like a mini-monk; oh I'm so nice, I'm a Buddhist. The point is to see our hate and attachment, how we use and consume each other.

I am told to imagine a father, mother, and child. Time passes; the parents die, the child grows up, marries, and has an infant. There is a battle with a dangerous enemy who dies.

Imagine you are the child-turned-adult, eating fish for lunch while breastfeeding your newborn. The dog nags for scraps. You feed it but then become impatient and kick it away. Boom: you realize the dangerous enemy has been reincarnated as your infant. Your father has been reincarnated as the fish you are eating. Your mother has returned as the kicked dog.

The dangerous enemy should be someone who arouses fear and hatred. I used bosses and exes, but Cheney? My brain made excuses: Haven't I had a crappy enough year? Hasn't he done enough?

Buddhist advice blogger Auntie Suvana provides a Cheney-specific visualization:

> Firstly, firmly establish in your mind the image of Richard sound asleep in giraffe pajamas. Richard is the name you gave him. You also gave him the pajamas. Notice the device inside his chest, poised to deliver a shock to restore the beat of his worn out, sad and violent heart. [E]ven though he has made many terrible mistakes, you can't help but love him. [Y]ou are always honest with him and encouraging him to do the right thing.[6]

Cheney in giraffe jammies was too much. I kept seeing his old bald head on a baby body, so I stuck with an anonymous baby. Alone with the glow of candles, Cheney's lips to my breast brings the visceral chill of the parent's worst nightmare.

Try it: your baby Cheney. You have given birth to Herculean levels of world damage. Nothing in your life matters more than raising this child to be a good person. The point is to love him. Love: dip your heart in lava. Do you think you are too good for this baby?

6 Auntie Suvana, "Ask Auntie Suvana: On Loving Dick Cheney," *Wild Mild Institute*, March 28, 2008.

But then I fall out of it, wheeling backward, feeling dirty and haunted and empty.

7.

I started looking for Cheney's childhood to get beyond the images from *The Omen* or *Rosemary's Baby*. Google found his football photo; he wore number sixteen for Natrona County High School in Casper, Wyoming. He's long-nosed and striking yet approachable, with a shaggy crew cut and a shy half-smile pulled up at the left-hand side of his innocent face.[7] His left hand is taped up loosely, and his helmet rests in his lap. His gangly limbs remind me of my own son, who looks frozen in photos because his natural state is motion. Cheney liked fishing and still does, just like my son.

Cheney and his wife Lynne, (née Vincent), met when they were fourteen; she was a cardigan-wearing blonde with a large, ruthless forehead and ice-blue eyes. She worked during the summers for Thomas Stroock, an oilman with massive connections at Yale who knew George H. W. Bush.[8] She impressed Stroock. Cheney was in, though of course he didn't know it yet.

8.

I had no Tom Stroock to help with private school, but cash came together. If I had been sent to Yale under the watchful eye of a benefactor, I believe I too would have imploded. At Carleton College in Minnesota, someone told me I had markers of the working class, the way I talked with my hand in front of my mouth and hid behind my hair. I protested weakly. But that was the culture I came from. I graduated, convinced that I was

7 "The Life and Career of Dick Cheney," *Washington Post,* June 22, 2007.
8 Stephen F. Hayes, *Cheney: The Untold Story of America's Most Powerful and Controversial Vice President.* New York: HarperCollins, 2009, 13.

stupid; I did fine on essays and assignments but felt as though I couldn't speak coherently. After college, I blundered on the East Coast, working low-paying jobs. I tried to stay away from the Midwest, which I identified as the problem inside me.

Cheney has a chip on his shoulder, or maybe the large chip has a small dangling Cheney. Maybe his axe to grind against the liberal elite was born at Yale. Cheney missed home, drank and partied, and lost his scholarship in 1960.[9] He left for home and climbed light poles as a card-carrying member of the International Brotherhood of Electrical Workers.[10] He later got an internship with a Republican representative almost by accident.

Then came the DUIs in 1962 and '63. I wonder if he and Lynne fought over his drinking or if it scared her. One theory posits that Lynne calls the shots and gives him structure, as often happens in codependent relationships.[11]

A posed photo from his junior year at the University of Wyoming—1964, the year he and Lynne married—shows no hint of a smile. His left eye looks gentle. The right one stares out coldly. In my notes, I wrote that I saw anger and a desire for revenge. Yet on second look, I see only a staring young man, filled out from his lanky high school days. His lips are full; you would have to describe this man as good-looking.

9.

After college, both Cheney and I began to mystify our parents. My Republican father tried to connect with his anarchist daughter, and I sprawled on my mom's bed as she patiently listened to me describe anarcho-syndicalism. Before Gulf

9 Ibid., p. 26.
10 John P. Briggs and J. P. Briggs II, "Dick Cheney's Psychology: Part II, The 'Attendant Lord,'" *TruthOut*, July 12, 2007.
11 Ibid.

War protests, the planning committee asked volunteers to get arrested. I wanted to, but I didn't. I couldn't ask my parents to pay bail when they didn't agree with anything I believed.

In 1991, the *Washington Post* profiled Cheney's parents. Cheney's father reported "mixed feelings" about the invasion of Kuwait, but they saw time collapse: "'Be sure to put in there that he was senior class president,' added his mother. 'And that he played football,' said her husband."[12] They cast back to what they knew, their boy.

10.

I like looking at some Cheney photos. The earlier ones show the polyester blends, longish haircuts, and boxy eyeglasses that mark my childhood in the 1970s and 1980s. Cheney served as President Gerald Ford's assistant, and my mom always loved Gerald Ford because he fell down so much. As a three-year-old, I fell down a lot too, so Ford and I were kindred spirits. I half-think my mom mostly loved Chevy Chase's impression of Ford falling down. She was a Republican because my father was. In the 1980s, you could even say my father and Cheney looked alike, with their suits and aquiline noses. But my dad ran a small business in Illinois while Cheney reached for the reins of the country.

I linger on the photos that show Cheney where he forgets his posture, where none of his limbs are suffused with cruelty. He is a man doing his job. He isn't yet hunched, and his hair isn't white. But hunching and white hair don't equal meanness; something else will change.

In a photo from 1980, Cheney and Lynne chase his kids in the family yard in McLean, Virginia. He was a US Representative from Wyoming at this point. His daughters, Elizabeth and Mary,

12 Ibid.; quotes from Phil McCombs, "The Unsettling Calm of Dick Cheney," *Washington Post*, April 3, 1991.

were ten and twelve; I was nine. The sides of his mouth turn up in happy symmetry, but he holds his torso and arms tightly, which makes the photo seem somewhat posed. He's no longer a man you would describe as attractive. He's balding and rounded, with a rim of hair around the back of his head.

11.

Cheney's heart betrays him, and my bones hatch rheumatoid arthritis. Meditation helps with the pain and anxiety, so I dive into the fish scenario: eating lunch, breastfeeding, feeding then kicking the dog. Yes, the baby is Cheney, his lips wet with milk.

One of my favorite photos of my son shows him sitting in his high chair, head half-covered with pureed sweet potato, even in his wisps of blonde hair. I'd sculpted his hair into a sweet-potato Mohawk. He leans with one arm reaching over the tray as if he's James Dean leaning out of a dragster. And he's got that smile, the same one, cocked up at the left. The smile of a charmer.

Breastfeeding, for me, was never a mystical, sleepy union. My wiry son was like a crazed ferret, and I had to lock him under my arm with what the lactation consultant called the "football hold," which must explain my son's passion for the NFL. His face slammed at me, desperate for milk, but his strong arms and legs flailed and I could barely hold on to him. I was covered in sweat at the end of each wrestling match. I imagine this is how it would be with Dick. There would be taking and giving but no merging.

I weaned my son very quickly after he tried his new teeth on my nipple. I pulled out to break the wet suction and yelled "Owww!" I checked for blood and clenched my jaw. He grinned cheekily, overjoyed at my reaction, as if to say, "I got you. This is me, separate, myself."

I weaned him because he was obviously done. He would slobber on my nipple, flubber at it, irritating the skin. Or he would suck on it weakly but turn his head to look toward interesting noises while pulling my nipple with his clenched mouth. I never mourned the loss of that contact; I wanted him to find his own sustenance. Separation was my goal for him. Remembering this helped with the Cheney meditation: I can feed this baby, and feeding is fine. But I don't have to cross into his soul.

One analysis describes Cheney's "dependency solution": he wants "powerful patrons [to] have confidence in him. He writes everyone else off."[13] Another profile of Cheney said that George H. W. Bush sought a guiding force for his son but "found a man who would make his son's dysfunctions worse."[14] A third analyst calls George W. Bush the "emotional bully" in the codependent relationship.[15] The younger Bush stated, "When you're talking to Dick Cheney, you're talking to me. When Dick Cheney's talking, it's me talking."[16]

12.

Cheney's stint as the Secretary of Defense matched my college years, 1989–1993. At twenty, I stood in the cold of a Minneapolis winter in a plaza surrounded with protest signs, sniffling. I did not know then that Cheney oversaw the first Gulf War. He and Rumsfeld learned from the Nixon-Vietnam era, and almost none of the demonstrations appeared on the evening news.

13 Ibid.
14 Ibid.
15 John P. Briggs and J. P. Briggs II, "Dick Cheney's Psychology: Part I, Almost Pleasantly Adrift," *TruthOut*, July 11, 2007.
16 Briggs and Briggs, part II, quote from *New Yorker*, May 7, 2007.

In 1989, he was offered a celebratory beer after winning his Pentagon post; he was rumored to have said, "Beer, hell. I'll have a double Scotch."[17] Maybe this fascinates me because I have history with substance abusers. The struggle in their darkened eyes is pain that can look and act like evil. Cheney supposedly carries a marked sense of "inner dread, gloom and fear."[18]

My first rounds of compassion meditation—and my immediate reason for becoming a Buddhist—were spurred by the pain of loving addicts. My meditation teacher told me not to envision absorbing the addiction when I did *tonglen*. I wished happiness for all beings; for the addicts, I hoped for the clarity to see their own agony.

People with substance abuse issues tend toward control, secrecy, and lies. Or maybe people with control issues sometimes drink. Cheney's hair turned white, his posture stooped, and his eyes squinted. By the time he got to the White House via the intoxicating wealth, power, and lack of oversight at Halliburton, he seemed to equate power with the ability to do whatever he wanted.[19]

A photo of Cheney in his kitchen in 2004 shows him talking on the phone to his daughter after George W. Bush was declared the winner of the presidential election. He leans on the counter, smiling, though his body and arms are curled together as if protecting something. The phone cord is wrapped around his body and held by his elbow. This is a touching detail: a corded phone in 2004. The kitchen is relatively small and beige, not huge and ostentatious. On the refrigerator door, magnets

17 Phil McCombs, "The Unsettling Calm of Dick Cheney; Defense's Civilian Chief and Seasoned Washington Hand, Playing It Cool," *Washington Post*, April 3, 1991.
18 Briggs and Briggs, part II.
19 He stamped much of his day-to-day correspondence as "Treated As: Top Secret/SCI," a designation referring to "sensitive compartmented information," usually used for hugely important government secrets. He added the "treated as" to make the argument that they were top secret, even though no one else had determined his memos to be of utmost national importance. He had his daily calendars and visitor logs destroyed. His general counsel argued that the vice president was not part of any branch of government and was therefore bound to no rules. Barton Gellman and Jo Becker, "'A Different Understanding with the President,'" *Washington Post*, June 25, 2007.

and maybe a spray of plastic alphabet letters hold family photos and a child's drawing. On the counter are a roll of paper towels, two bottles of wine, and a toaster oven.[20] This is what I would call his evil period. He looks flushed; his mouth is making the slit shape of a smile. His eyes look elsewhere, as if his brain is detached. I realize I cannot know what is in his head.

13.

I am on a short plane ride by myself. Because the rheumatoid arthritis pain is bad again and I don't have the energy to read, I go to Cheney. As I begin with the baby, I realize I have never thought about my potential power over him. In this scenario, I am huge and could crush his small body. It has never tempted me.

I must pull up my shirt and let this creature find sustenance without judgment. But wait, this is a fussy baby—of course. And so I envision patting the back of this cosmically whiny baby, doing the baby dance, singing "sshhhh—ssshhhh—shhh—it's gonna be all right—shhhh," waiting for the gas to die down, hoping to soothe this jangled nervous system.

We each have a will like the third rail of a subway train, and I feel this baby's hot anger. I have felt my son's own acute frustration with limits and the rules of life. We all want dominion. This baby I have borne is going to plug its ego into the huge, electrified tracks of the train that slammed into Iraq as Afghanistan and Saudi Arabia slammed into us, as we slammed into the USSR, as the USSR slammed into Afghanistan. Even wishing harm on this baby Cheney won't unplug the generations of rage and desire he has dutifully served. I have a right to be horribly angry at him, even if he were my child. I have a right to disagree.

20 "The Life and Career of Dick Cheney," *Washington Post,* June 22, 2007.

As I imagine holding this wiry ferret baby against my thighs, I realize I can hold his body, but I have no business or ability to touch the live third rail of his soul. Putting your hands on someone else's third rail results in instant death. Cheney has plugged into the electricity he sought. He is on fire with it. This baby is on fire, on a powerful train that has led to destruction. I know this baby rage wants to annihilate me, too, but the one peace I see is that I can step back from that rail to see what it has consumed. It has devoured my imaginary son for its own heat and power.

TARGET, SAVED

Towel pinched up beneath my armpits, I held the purple cotton shirt, looking for the tag and the way in, all those necessary road maps. Its thinness and pilled surface looked like time, like a child's touch-softened blanket. The shirt hung like a flag, uninflated and at arm's length, its yoke stretched between my fingers, and my gut twisted: *You are from the bad time.*

The shirt just wanted a normal life after its birth in a sweatshop, an Easter egg born for the Gap from the hands of babies. Clothing must shudder at clearance sales, except for those shirts that long for riffraff and adventure, like me. Clearance is when the desperate come in. No, the desperate pretenders meandering through their lives in search of labels and fabrics to make the ugly at home at least have edges that match with other people's edges.

Here I go again. I promised myself, getting my coffee, wearing this shirt, stretching the armholes to put on deodorant, that I wouldn't get lost in my own icing. I would just say it. The problem, as always, is me: I recently crowed and shone two whole days after replacing the metal cabinet handles in the kitchen. I thrilled at the massive change from such a small decision and said proudly, "It doesn't take much to make me happy." And he (my husband, Cliff, not the way-back man) said, "Maybe that's been the problem." And we laughed with the rue of the saved, but he was right. I have always been too good at squeezing joy from turnips and stones.

The shirt—actually most of my clothing—stretches its history into the heart of a timeline anchored with livid, steaming pain. I lived the days and nights in them, and they hid me the best they could. They became my outer layer, so undoubtedly, they also felt themselves targets. That idea makes shopping for clothes at Target slightly less fun; best not think of that again.

Drawstring yoga pants from that certain moment when I was wild with desperation and abandoned. The extravagance, in our poverty, of a nightgown with flowers I bought for retail price, not on clearance at all, for either $14 or $19 right after the way-back man started rehab. Every time I put it on, I remember the wave of unbridled rage that came out from a deep place of lava where I only expected relief. That flowered nightgown (Target) and, later, the flowered bedspread (Target too) each spoke of a future I imagined in which I could sleep untouched. It took such hard living to reach this point, to where I sleep safely under the flowered bedspread every night, its surface softened with washing.

I keep the navy-blue, thrift-store flannel robe and many other thrift-store finds because they are not yet worn out. Thrift-store clothing breathes Goodwill like a Buddhist, wishing you well despite the wreckage that passes the aisles. Thrift-store clothing holds you, comforts you with the other lives it has seen and can't talk about. It says, *I know. I have seen worse.* You hope it has seen worse so your life doesn't seem so bad. I love the slight disinfectant chemical smell that's hard to get out of Goodwill clothing. I shouldn't. But to me it says, *Remember the others who passed this way. You are not alone.*

Poor purple retail shirt from the Gap who I castigate for being from the bad time, knowing I could say the same of myself: You know I don't mean it. You know what I know: that writing it down stretches it further and further away, makes it abstract like the lines of a tape measure spooling outward, lineated, each tick mark bearing not a number but the same phrase—*no longer, no further*—over and over. Our dear, steadfast household objects break through days and remain themselves in my house where I left them last, to rear up out of drawers and closets like zombies or skeletons. God, they get right in my face with their rolling, shining, manic eyes, their threats and winces and muttered profanities.

No, not the things. The shirts and the books and each fucking flowerpot, they don't do that. That's my neurons, sifting. The things bring back the moments of specific garage-sale peace. The things all signal salvation. I cared enough about myself on that one day to buy that orange shirt. I had enough hope to prize that Audrey Hepburn pink raincoat from a tangle of clothing on a flatbed truck in the August heat of a Georgia scrub-grass yard sale. I scraped together many, many threads that are still with me, and I am no longer a target.

THE TIDE IS HIGH: MIDWESTERN DIRGE, 2019

I take the flat edge of Illinois and cut myself, WXRT west over the DuPage River, Tears for Fears and the rusted bridges, REM singing, "What's the Frequency, Kenneth?" in the flatness. Spindly wild sunflowers in the ditches, and the sky is gray as lint while Puerto Ricans die after a hurricane and the *New York Times* wonders how we wrest the nuclear codes out of a dangerous pair of tiny hands. Tom Petty is dead, but Bruce and Barack are not, not yet. Not yet. I'm driving my mom's car west to Iowa, and I never had a car this nice when I lived here, so I turn the radio up loud enough to feel the bass in my shins, and I think about the time I've already served, fearing nuclear war in the apocalyptic flatness of the eighties. The sky here gives the illusion of being able to see forever, but really, you can't. Overpasses punctuate the highway like clicks of a metronome. This is where I learned that loud guitar was the only covered medical expense. Twin silos. Tree on the horizon like the last woman standing. My mom told me this morning that they are scooping out the coal from right beneath a Pennsylvania town. They truck in water in bottles. Hitches and chains, we don't care what we sell, sell it fucking all. I picked up Lincoln on the roadside with hollow eyes, and he said, "Just keep going west, I don't care where we go, just get me the fucking hell out of here," and I said, "The West is on fire."

Out in the sea of corn past the range of WXRT, I raise my hand to the dash, pointing to the horizon with my middle finger, pressing "Seek" to scroll through the numbers and the blanks between stations. Out here it is still the 1980s, and Guns N' Roses tells me to be patient. *Seek, seek, seek.*

My son saw Eminem's tribute to Colin Kaepernick's raised fist before I did, and I trust that if he's not reading the headlines, Instagram is at least giving him the pulse. I plow the highway west like stitching a yellow seam on gray fabric, like a saw blade cutting the country in two. This place taught me to appreciate a palette of brown and gray, the strips of gold and blue like a Rothko.

I learned American history from a scrawl of graffiti on the northbound Dan Ryan, south of the Robert Taylor homes, "Amerikkka," and mulled over that for decades. There are white people whose only indignity ever is a TSA pat-down. I pass Sterling, near the birthplace of Ronald Reagan, whose last revenge is that some would be glad to have him now, who whisper this is also his fault. He was a liberal when he left this place.

"Trust Jesus" sprayed on every concrete overpass, though the words look a little faded now. I still can't figure out what I love about the blank amnesia of this place, which is no worse than any other place in the country where "fun is spelled with two Ns now," or so the radio tells me. I'm not an idiot—I know that art won't change a thing, it's just the life support we need to keep going through the song's next measure. Remember the Cold War, guys? Remember when you were filled with fury and this defined your Rambo selves? Russia won. Russia won. Today, you don't even care that Russia won.

Outside of Peoria, the radio announcer says that the Wheel of Meats comes on at 9:40 every weekday morning, and one lucky caller spins to get a choice cut from the local deli. AC/DC is back in black, same as it ever was. Listen, you guys, my sister had thyroid cancer, what a preexisting condition, but now she's got Australian citizenship because she used to work over there. Trump just tried to cut health care so she's going back with my two nephews. Bye again, bye bye again, my mother's brokenhearted, but America could literally kill her. But I can't think about that now because I'll throw up from the sadness, so I just look at the road.

Nothing but cock rock, three decades old, and religion on the radio now. Passing an oversized load, I am pushing "Seek" with my middle finger and kind of working myself into a panic attack. It must be the atmosphere, it must be too much time to think, it must be the kind of Jesus that never spoke to me. Lincoln is fading out to blue like Obi-Wan, going back to whatever shell he sleeps in, reachable only at 867-5309.

This place opens like a picture book, the grimmest picture book in grays and browns, but, God, doesn't it show you what's in your soul? And then it shows you a field of new wheat, lime green and gold like the promised land, only poisoned. The landscape stays the same, and my mind cycles from beauty to horror and back.

Yeah, I've been a student of classic rock meditation since I was born, in the monastery of the highway, navigating among the sundown towns that don't know their own stories. I always liked the name Rock Island because it implies a body of water somewhere, the rock a place to stand.

What kind of music is this if the cars on the highway are notes on the bars to a song? The midwestern dirge or monastic chant. Where's my goddamn Tom Petty? I can feel when I'm getting closer to Iowa because the land starts to ripple a little and the clouds hang low like heavy udders.

The corn is dead, and I rip through it, past the long scar of my own psyche that stripes north-south along Illinois's long body, and I am into someone else's landscape, and I put myself back together as a person.

And I wish Lincoln well, along with whoever he is visiting now, and I hope all our patron saints are having good mornings this Thursday, and I pray we get another chance. Squeeze comes on the radio singing "Tempted" and encouraging me to flee. Illinois is like a drunken flashback unhinged from time, and I am crying to static and Aerosmith. No, I don't put music on my phone, it's all filled with Buddhist podcasts so I can learn to drive the flatness inside me, so I can learn to watch the weather as it rolls. I turn off the radio and the Buddha says, "Hi," and, "Why the fuck were you doing that to yourself?" And I say, "It's the eighties, I caught me some *samsara*, no escape." And the Buddha says, "Karma isn't punishment. But that doesn't mean it won't hurt." Construction now near East Moline, and orange barrels line the roadsides. Once, on a long ride with my son, a single-mother pilgrimage, I told the restless boy that each orange barrel had a name. And so we named them as we rolled—*Carl, Sharon*—and I'm sure of only a few things in life, but I am sure that this is true. Mighty Mississippi, forgive us, we know not what we do.

The only writing residencies I've ever done have had a steering wheel and rest stops every hour. My son is midwestern-born, and he wants to move back, and I haven't told him it's like growing up Catholic, like a wound that murmurs when you want to get some sleep. The dragging screech of wipers across the half-dry windshield, the smell of wet asphalt, incense—all the things you shouldn't love but do. And out here it's suddenly obvious, why you have a weird roadside synesthesia, why every emotion calls up asphalt, why the index of your soul is keyed to intersections rather than faces.

Lincoln's back suddenly, hologram-sharp. "Drive westward, ho," he says with a smirk.

"You can't talk to me like that," I say to him.

He smiles and says, "I can now. We've reached peak awful, didn't you hear?"

"You're not real," I tell him

He reaches over and puts a finger through my arm.

"Neither are you."

I want coffee, chocolate, or a cigarette, something that tastes like earth so I can start burying myself in advance. It's only flyover country if you're not tough enough to drive right through the center channel of your own mind, cross the corpus callosum. The baddest motherfuckers like me do it in silence. But even we, the few, the proud, the brave, are scared of where eighties rock will take us in our minds.

Now they don't want us to kill our babies early and quick. They'd rather wait and draw it out as long as possible, stretch the pain through their childhoods, sadism in slow-motion. They'd rather smile and make us watch as they do it.

"I'm in a dark place," I say to Lincoln.

"So was I," he says, "but now I am free."

I realize I've been driving for three hours and I've only heard the music of men. The pelts of unspooled tires litter the roadside. Then Blondie comes on and sings about the rising tide and not giving up.

And suddenly, leering Lincoln is gone. Someone has written "Trump!" in the grime on the back of the semi in front of me, and I wish I knew what those letters meant to that person. I pass the truck. I realize what "love it or leave it" means. It doesn't mean "Have a great life in Canada." It means "Die, and we'll even help you to do it."

Christ does open-heart surgery on a billboard. Mist hangs onto the roll of a crew-cut field. Mountains, fine. The oceans, yes. But nobody could paint this pink, gold, and brown flatness complete with high tension wires and a turquoise trailer. All this open space without enough room for conversation. I love this place and it doesn't love me back.

STARBUCKS AND SHIPWRECKS

Jen and I sit at Starbucks, and we talk about the men who shine.

They come in with their knuckle ink and neck tattoos, and they order tall triple-shot cappuccinos. We know them like a compass needle knows north, like Ahab knew the whale. We love them, these men who were lost at sea and decided to save themselves, who decided to let themselves be lifted out of the drink.

If you don't know how to spot a man like this, you might look at him and think he's a little weathered, like maybe he spent a lot of time outside. He holds his paper cup like any other man—but different. He breathes like any other man—but different. A man in recovery sometimes looks like this: hands and skin so worn that you know he has at some point been to the ER for coughing up blood or with his face smashed in. Sometimes you see it merely around the eyes: a triple layer of crow's feet or lids that have closed with a thousand-hour sleep.

They confound, and that is how you know. Mixed with the signals of worn-to-hell-and-back are the signs of forward motion: shoulders down and relaxed, pink in the cheeks, a clean jacket, or a book. It's in the eyes, the Buddha-look of a man who sits with craving living inside his skull and decides, today, not to act on it. To make eye contact and see other humans in the way that, honestly, few humans can bear to see each other. To watch that fire burn and tend it with the help of his team.

Jen and I, we've been with these men. And we find it hard to explain the body's intuition. We love them best, maybe because they've broken our hearts.

———————

Decades ago, I used to hate them, the druggies and drunks and homewreckers, even the sober ones. I could not abide a minute, a glance, a polite nod hello. I slipped past them at church entrances on my way to my meeting for loving addicts and alcoholics, just down the hall from their meeting. I wanted to retch at the smell of their cigarette smoke, the orange glowing dots moving up and down in the night as they sucked in nicotine before going inside to inhale hope.

That was the time in my life where I said I didn't want to read *Moby-Dick* because I already had a few too many dicks in my life.

I shook and cowered and post-post-traumatic-stressed and cried and fluttered and could not look anyone in the eye. I was a shaking, rigid, terrified sparrow-squirrel sobbing on the subway. I was a wrecked collateral-damage harpy shrew. I was turned to stone and salt.

I thawed.

———————

Last month after a meeting, a guy came up to me wearing marks on his face that betrayed a certain geology of the soul.

His skin seemed a little more tightly stretched around his skull, his eyes a little deep-set in his head. His clothing seemed as though—in a way I can barely explain—it had just been put on him, layered over another, scarier life from which he had just emerged. All of these survivors: they wake up, see demons, shower, and stride into the world fresh and yet super-scathed, perfectly aware of what they left behind. They are rooted in their seats, where they are. They turn their heads to look at you and they are *on,* shining like a second-chance Icarus who has to come to Daedalus and said, "Dad, I fucked up." They should be dead.

Swamp. Skin. Icarus: all this in a half-second when this man smiled at me.

"Do I know you from the other rooms?" he asked, his eyes both dark and clear. By "other rooms," he meant, are you a "double winner"? Are you both scorched by another person's addiction *and also at the same time* a survivor of your own?

That's what some people carry.

"No, just this one," I said, meaning that I'm not an addict. "But I look like a lot of people." I smiled and hugged him. "Have a good week."

Fifteen years ago, I would have seen it as an insult, but last week, I gloated. I savored it for the ride home and a few days afterward. This was a chip I had not realized I could collect. I didn't know I wanted it: that someone had seen me and thought, *There is a spine forged from fighting monsters.*

Some people don't like the word "addict" and "alcoholic" because they find those words pejorative and damning. People I love in recovery know that calling themselves out with words like this is a way to keep hold of life above the ground.

It's not an insult. It's a crown, a spear, a scrimshaw carved in bone.

Jen and I meet at Starbucks to work her step, which means she answers questions in a book that we say is annoying. By annoying, we mean that it is so direct and honest that it makes us hate ourselves as a route to give up the hate and love ourselves instead. We lean over the book and howl with laughter at our own matching, messed-up histories, the likes of which inevitably make the coffee drinkers at the tables on either side of us stop and stare. The point—the desperate jewel—has been to get to where we don't care who hears our deepest secrets in a Starbucks.

We're here at Starbucks, maybe because Starbuck is the chief mate in *Moby-Dick,* guiding the *Pequod* toward Captain Ahab's fatal desire for the whale, his craving for craving itself, his desire to extract and burn the essence of another. Starbuck, a Quaker, is the only character who stands up to Ahab. Did you know that Perth, the ship's blacksmith, is an alcoholic whose wife and child had fled his drunken rages? Perth forges the harpoon to spear the white whale. Did you know that Herman Melville was raised by a brutal alcoholic and that, after his child died, he turned to alcohol himself?

Herman M. died a half century too soon to meet Bill W.

Jen tells me she'd been sitting at a table in the back, where she overheard a guy on the phone. He spoke a few key words, maybe "higher power" or "personal inventory" or "amends." She said hi to the guy, told him she was eavesdropping, and they chatted about program.

"An older guy," she said. "You just know sometimes."

I nodded. "Ahh, those AA old-timers, they're so great, no

bullshit." I pictured a plaid shirt, remains of a beer gut, gimlet eye to pierce the hide of a white whale.

She shook her head and laughed. "No, this one was dapper. True sense of style."

"Coke?" I wondered.

We laughed, burning the essence of darkness for light. We think we know our men, this universe of them, how a man who's been to meth and back might shine, what they look like polished up and saved. We play that we can predict the traces of a chemical on a soul, though we know these images deceive. We've seen the imprint on skin and teeth and scalp and faces, and yet we know enough to know our guesses always fall short. We only know we love them, the Starbucks, the first mates of the shipwrecked and the saved.

THE MAGPIES OF INDUSTRY

Our senses collect what they see and make a little world inside us, an amulet of place to anchor our roaming bodies. I believe my amulet, my geographical compass, is tuned to the heartbreak love of weathered, rusted industry: the palimpsest of layered paint on brick, the corrugated metal of a boxy warehouse, the gravel and grit of asphalt, the gray of smokestacks and pipes and concrete viaducts. We don't choose our parents, and we don't choose our first landscapes.

When you drive toward Chicago from the south through the sweep of Gary and Hammond, Indiana, you see the flat sides of the old steel mills, some still burning but most just catching the light of the setting sun in their windows. Those buildings are a color that changes with the midwestern sky, orange to lilac to gray. They were made in one color, but time has made them mottled and is taking them back, bit by bit. It is the oldness, too, that I love. Their faces are splashed with bits of paint, applied and then washed and bleached and worn away, leaving an industrial collage that is in all honesty a painting made by humans in collaboration with the earth itself. I wish there were a name for this gallery, these faded splotched walls of stone and brick and steel and paint.

The hand of my early travels stretches far and wide across the upper and lower Midwest, returning always via I-80 or I-55 to New Lenox, Illinois, New Lenox, set next to the once-steel city of Joliet. We traveled for my parents' work; we traveled south to my grandparents, whose stories sung of *work, work, work.* And so I saw in the buildings that housed work a kind of gray church. In the beginning, I wasn't drawn to the ugly out of a contrarian stance. In the beginning, I saw the backs and ends of things: loading dock, hand-truck dolly, open mouth of a truck, plume of smoke.

I don't have to face the same loading dock every day. Or rather, I do, but when I enter the loading dock of my academic building, I go into an academic office where my mind gets to wander, perched atop the narrow bones of my vertebrae. I don't have to haul metal, shift gears, move steel, or smell the same rusty, grease-tinged stink of the same place. Like any other worker, I have to listen to the same people complaining for twenty years. But I can hide, and no one times my lunch breaks, and if my body aches at the end of the day, it is from inactivity instead of from burning overuse. I have been a tourist in the landscape that made me.

Another human's heart might sing for mountains. I know so many people who have left an ugly place. They walk new paths, breathe new air, and let a beautiful place scribe new marks on their soul. I find that as admirable as any other way to survive, but it is not the only way. In some ways, my impulse to love the worn and broken is the best part of me.

If I die in traffic on the highway, it won't be because of my cell phone. It will be near Exit 27 of I-95 in Bridgeport, Connecticut. Near that stretch of elevated road, old brick buildings hulk, many of them a century old or more, the factories that once made corsets and gramophones and buttons and light switches. They are now empty shells, all grown with weeds and pinked with the force of the sun. I have wandered in them and touched their animal hides. In traffic, I stare at them like friends, and I love them like Monet loved his haystacks, I suppose. In each light, they cast a different color, and I notice the tide of graffiti washed over with the city's black paint, the back and forth of urban surf.

I love those buildings so much that my love has grown complicated and fractal and tendrilled, so I can't say in a simple way why I love them. I love them for their endurance and for their loneliness. I sometimes think of the workers who used to work there, all long dead, and I suppose my labor-union sensibilities would put me on their sides, but my love is not tactical, not strategic. I love the things that "earth has given and human hands have made," that phrase from the Catholic Mass also scribed over and over into my soul. I love the reminders of workers past because the history of workers is so often completely erased, written nowhere, while the history of singular wealthy white men tends to cram the bookshelves in flaccid florid detail. I suppose in loving these buildings— these mountains of industry lit by the sun and the moon and shadowed by shifting clouds—I am loving the strands of what made me and what made so many, the men and women who went to work and whose names grace no monument. These buildings on the landscape—built so strong it would be dangerous or expensive to take them down, or contaminated so thoroughly they must be left alone—stand for the work that made them and the work they once held.

I am nostalgic for a time when industrial jobs were plentiful, an economic gene copied forward out of the Midwest's fading industrial greatness, the last stand of the unionized middle class, the downsized transition to service industry and information superhighway, gigged and temped and contracted out. I am an information worker who hearkens back with a ruined nostalgia to an assembly line that often broke the bodies of men and women; I ran away into the alphabet. I love a warehouse because I love the look and feel of jobs, employment, the hope of family stability. The jobs went and the unions took hit after hit in a civil war or self-sabotage we don't mention much because we are still living it. I love a warehouse, its profile captured in steel and brick, as a family album. I love the labor history that my college education pointed me toward but that only marks my body in subtle ways, on the inside of my skull and spirit. I learned about radical social movements by researching with hands soft and quick on the keyboard. It's all backward, like using the handle of a shovel to try to dig a hole for a grave.

———————

I lurk the online discussion boards where people write about weird walks across the industrial palm of a city and strange finds in urban geography. I see the same sweep of awe in a cathedral's nave as in a long, tall warehouse. In both long spaces, humans were told to put their heads down in deference to a greater power, and yet the walls themselves are a testament above all else to the flawed human heart and the strength of our hands.

Urban lofts are expensive and yet lovely for their exposed brick and timbers, for the big yawning windows that were once the only way to capture light by which to stitch and weave and stamp. I can't afford a loft anywhere, but like those loft-dwellers, I love the look of the rough past I didn't have to live. Or maybe in the old handmade things, I can almost see the aged faces and hands of the people that made them, and I want those people around me, somehow, to have their lights burn still.

If I were from the coast or the mountains, I would pick up shells and bits of wood. I like to do that on a seaside walk, but I am an industrial magpie. When I walk a faded street, I look for bits of smashed and rusted metal in the gravel, and when I find them, I pick them up and examine them like fossils for the work and time recorded there. We who are from metal and brick feel an ache for these pieces of meteor and stardust collected into deposits of ore, of clay and mud, which are also of the earth and the space and the dreams that made us.

ACKNOWLEDGMENTS

"Flying the Flannel" first appeared in *Vela*. An earlier version of "My Men" appeared as a single essay in *Fourth Genre,* as did "Homage to a Bridge." "All in the Family" first appeared in *Learning to Glow: A Nuclear Reader* (University of Arizona Press). "Love and Industry: A Midwestern Workbook" first appeared in *Terrain: A Journal of the Built and Natural Environments.* "Chicagoland" first appeared in the Belt anthology *Rust Belt Chicago,* edited by Martha Bayne. "Miller High Life: The Champagne of Beers" appeared in the *Pinch.* "Questions about the Lakeview Café" was created from an essay of the same name that appeared in *Sub-Lit* and "Only Money," which appeared in the *Florida Review.* "Land of Infinite David" appeared in the *Crab Orchard Review.* "Glass Beads" appeared in the *Baltimore Review.* "Goat-Baby" appeared in *Literary Mama* and in *Mama, PhD: Women Write about Motherhood and the Academic Life* (Rutgers University Press). "Greetings from Divorceland!" appeared in *Mamapalooza.* "Starbucks and Shipwrecks" appeared in *Creative Nonfiction*, and "Breastfeeding Dick Cheney" appeared in *Creative Nonfiction* and in the anthology *True Stories, Well Told: From the First 20 Years of Creative Nonfiction* (Creative Nonfiction). "The Magpies of Industry" appeared in the anthology *Deep Beauty: Experiencing Wonder When the World is On Fire* (Woodhall Press).

Thank you to Anne Trubek and Mike Jauchen at Belt for seeing potential and a whole in these pieces, and to Mike for your insightful edits that helped stitch these essays into a book. Thank you to the editors who accepted this work and worked with me to develop it, including the departed and beloved Michael Steinberg at *Fourth Genre,* who gave vital encouragement when I was an MFA student. A deep thank you to the thoughtful, expert, and ever-encouraging Hattie Fletcher and the rest of the former staff of *Creative Nonfiction* for your steadfast support and amazing work; you've been a cornerstone for essayists. Thank you to the too-soon-departed Jon Tribble at the *Crab Orchard Review*; Simone Gorrindo and Amanda Giracca at *Vela*; John Bradley, who worked with me in 1995 via looseleaf paper sent via snail mail for my first anthology publication, "All in the Family"; Simmons Buntin at *Terrain*; Barbara Westwood Diehl at the *Baltimore Review*; Lisa Roney at the *Florida Review*; Martha Bayne; and Rosemary Winslow and Catherine Lee at Woodhall Press. Thank you to Caroline Grant and the whole *Literary Mama* crew for giving me a literary home when I was reeling as a young mom. It's such a pleasure to look at how the web of friendship has been built through lines of text and encouragement and connection. Thank you also for the encouragement, support, and love: my parents; Glenn, Meg, and Sarah; Nicole, Tim, Wiley, and Nathaniel; and to anybody who's picked up this book. Thank you to my dear and long list of friends, and especially to Jenny, Brooke, Nicole, Monica, Kathy, Nalini, Barbara, and Elizabeth, who loved me through the living of these words. Thanks to everyone who fights for the rights of workers and the right to choose or not choose parenthood. And thank you to Cliff and Ivan, whose love sustains me.

ABOUT THE AUTHOR

Sonya Huber's books include *Voice First: A Writer's Manifesto*, the award-winning collection *Pain Woman Takes Your Keys and Other Essays from a Nervous System*, and *Supremely Tiny Acts: A Memoir in a Day*. Many of her books, including *Opa Nobody* and *Cover Me: A Health Insurance Memoir*, address labor and social movements, and she cofounded the Columbus, Ohio, chapter of Jobs with Justice as well as the 2017 online Disability March. Born and raised in Illinois, she has worked in the nonprofit sector and in social work. She received the Kiplinger Fellowship in Public Interest Journalism and her MFA from the Ohio State University. She now teaches at Fairfield University in Connecticut.